PRAISE FOR *RICH AS F*CK:*

"The book is the bible on money." —ANDREA CROWDER

"No one is a clearer channel on money than Amanda Frances." —DANIELLE BIGBY

"This is not just a book, but literally a resource that will change your perspective on money." —CHELSEA NEWMAN

"This book is fucking fire. And so many quotable words and relatable thoughts. Thank you for pushing through, Amanda. This shit is a gift. I'm walking away feeling full of self-love, acceptance and inspiration." —ADRIANNA ARIAS

"I didn't want it to end." —KAYLA RAE

"Let me just move the surprise cash I received in the mail and the unexpected payments in my business that appeared out of thin air out of the way so I can focus on telling you this: GET THIS BOOK. Amanda will teach you to overflow with abundance. What do you have to lose?" —LIZ BROUSSEAU

"Amanda's teachings are worth their weight in gold. Her practical yet spiritual teachings will get you hooked on manifestation and wealth creation. This was the missing piece I needed to scale my business and repair my relationship with money. I will be forever grateful to you, Amanda. You've completely changed how I view and feel about money. Life has never been so abundant." —CARLY ANNA

"You should only read this if you want more money in your reality." —SHAUNNA LEE

"Since finding Amanda's work, I have paid off over 90K in credit card debt and created a nest egg of over $150K, all in the span of a few years! Unsurprisingly, this book is insanely powerful. During the chapter 2 homework, I wrote that I wanted to be featured in *Forbes*. My first book was featured on their best of 2019 list three days later." —MEGAN SADD

"This book is THE money oracle. All women need to read it. Forget every other wealth or money manifestation book. This book is all you will ever need. After reading the first three chapters, £5K practically dropped out of the sky for me and it's been dropping ever since. The homework at the end of each chapter really gets you to go deep on your money beliefs and shift that story!"
—LEANNE MACDONALD

"This book is phenomenal. Thank you for being a true beacon of self-love and acceptance who lights up the way for others." —LAURIE FRANCIS

"I started *Rich as F*ck* and immediately got four referrals creating my best month yet and booking $20,000-$30,000 months for the next three months. And I just received a random $30,000 check in the mail from an uncle I haven't talked to in ten years. I am religiously going through your journal exercises from the book and doing the recommended daily assignments from chapter 4!" —ANONYMOUS

"I read the first chapter and slept well for the first time in weeks. High-vibe money dreams." —DAWN PETERSON

"I am left feeling more inspired after reading Amanda's words, and more certain that money mindset work is so damn important." —EMILY KING

"I am so energized and happy since coming across Amanda Frances. Every single day, my energy around money gets better and better. My life continually improves, and I attract more and more money ALL THE TIME in larger and larger quantities. Thank you so much for helping me shift my paradigms around money. Straight game changer for my life." —BUMI TULLY

"No one explains it like Amanda does. This book is amazing. It is the healing work our planet needs. Amanda is doing so much generational healing in the realm of money. She is so raw and vulnerable. Truly a gift. Thank you for sharing the magic." —SONIA GODFREY

"*Rich as F*ck* has shown me a new belief system and way of being in the world. My thoughts and beliefs are now in alignment with what I desire. I talk more about my desires and rarely even notice struggles because my mind's always shifting. If something challenging or seemingly shitty happens, I can so easily find God's higher reasoning that was actually supporting my growth. I've never been this trusting, optimistic, certain, and ready for more. So much love for *Rich As F*ck* and Amanda's gorgeous journaling questions. Thank you. Thank you. Thank you." —DIANA MITCHELL

"This is an incredible book. I cannot wait to read over and over again. Thank you so much for your gift. I'm going to keep on keeping on and building my dream." —AMY HYDE

"I am just loving this book. It resonates so much and gets me so excited!" —MISHELLE BEE

"The chapters blew my mind. I have such a clear feeling of what it was like living my dream." —TYRA WEITMAN-SOET

"I just read the last chapter of this incredible book! I know this book will bring so much clarity and inspiration to all who read it." —TARA CALLAHAN

"This is powerful, beautiful, honest, filled with love and lots of understanding. I love this book. I love the way you decided to do you, write, create and deliver it!" —SARAH ANN

"Phenomenal, Amanda. How divine, adding sections on the important lessons that came through this year, with the fucking PANDEMIC (and money mindset), and inclusivity (and money mindset). I'm so happy for you, Love. And happy for us, and everyone who's going to be served by your offering!" —VICKY AUF DER MAUER

"*Rich As F*ck* is so insightful! Get ready to rethink your entire life." —RAINE BOYD

"The first chapter was LIFE. I can FEEL how GOOD this book is going to be." —ALYSA NUNEZ

"This book is what I needed. Major breakthroughs." —KAYSE BLAIR

RICH AS F*CK

MORE MONEY THAN YOU
KNOW WHAT TO DO WITH

AMANDA FRANCES

Amanda Frances Inc.
LOS ANGELES, CALIFORNIA

Amanda Frances Inc.
www.amandafrances.com

Copy editing by Stephanie Gunning, Cara Lockwood, and Rebecca Caccavo
Book production by Stephanie Gunning

Special discounts are available on quantity purchases by corporations, associations, and others. For details, contact the publisher.

Library of Congress Control Number 2020924679

Rich as F*ck / Amanda Frances — 1st ed.

ISBN 978-1-7353751-0-6 (paperback)
ISBN 978-1-7353751-1-3 (kindle ebook)
ISBN 978-1-7353751-2-0 (epub ebook)

To my little sister, Andrea.

It's only right that my first official book be dedicated to you, too. I love you.

CONTENTS

FOREWORD

When your friend and fellow entrepreneur earns millions of dollars a year doing what she loves on her own terms, you listen to her, and you learn from her. And then you share her with everyone you know. This is why I couldn't be more thrilled that this book is now in your hands.

I have a vivid memory of the first time Amanda and I met in person. I'm not sure who connected us or how, but we had been orbiting in each other's universes for some time before we sat down for coffee and had a real conversation. It was a humid day late in the summer in New York City. The kind of day where the air hangs heavy, life feels slower, and a thick breeze from a filthy subway train whizzing by feels luxurious. I was on my way to a SoulCycle class in downtown Brooklyn, and Amanda and I had made plans to meet at Le Pain Quotidien while she was in town for an afternoon snack and a couple of lattes.

It was on that warm summer afternoon that Amanda informed me she was writing a book. As an author, I was ecstatic that she was taking her message "on the road" and making her heart and expertise available on a grand scale. Let's be real: Amanda is expensive. Her courses are a few thousand dollars, and her private coaching is the cost of a down payment on a small home. And she is worth every penny and then some. But the fact that she's now making herself and her knowledge accessible to millions of more people through this book is a testament to the fact that she is dedicated to seeing *all* women thrive.

It would be years after that day when Amanda announced her plans to write this book that I'd find myself writing the foreword for it. In that time, I have watched her evolve into a force to be reckoned with. Not to say she wasn't a force before, but she has elevated her business to a level that expands far beyond what I've seen in the standard world of online coaching. If you've followed her for any length of time, you know exactly what I'm talking about.

Amanda Frances gives a fuck. She walks her walk, she cares deeply and genuinely about seeing other women succeed, and she is beyond generous with her content, her wisdom, and her energy. And I should know. I've not only followed her work for years, but we've cultivated a friendship over time. I've also done her courses and implemented her strategies to great success in my own life.

I now understand why it's taken her a few years to put this book together. It's because the universe had bigger plans for all of us. Life had to align in such a way where this book would be needed now more than *ever*. We are in new territory. The game has changed. Opportunities are boundless, and you now have access to the best possible teacher to lead you through the process of being, doing, and receiving everything you want.

As a fellow entrepreneur who also believes in boldly and generously supporting other women entrepreneurs, I recently had Amanda on my podcast, *Style Your Mind*. She said something that gave me chills: "The divine understanding is that well-resourced women can do some good shit in this world. Money amplifies people."

All women are meant to be wealthy. Regardless of our background, our past, our race, our previous mistakes, our education, the current state of our bank account, our parents, or their parents. We're meant to make an impact in whatever way lights us up. We're meant to experience a deep sense of freedom, give ourselves and those we love whatever we want, and more. And until we get our money mentality in check and know exactly how to call in that wealth, we'll remain stuck. And there's nothing empowering about being stuck.

I recommend approaching this book with an open mind and an open heart. Amanda's philosophies around money are *radical, spiritual,* and *powerful.* From understanding that money is unlimited, to healing your past beliefs, to clearing the path so you can quantum leap into the next, most abundant version of yourself, Amanda is not your average money expert.

But she's the only one that matters right now.

It's time to drop the fear, guilt, and other bullshit stories we have around earning and receiving money. Money helps us go bigger, be more, and do more. Money helps us change the world. Period. Full stop.

If you're in a funky place with money, if your beliefs about what you can have, earn, and save need to be shifted, if your energy around money needs an overhaul, then you've landed in the right place.

As Amanda says, "Remember: life is meant to be good." It's time to drop the struggle, babe. It's time to be rich as fuck.

—Cara Alwill,
bestselling author, success coach, and
host of the *Style Your Mind* podcast

INTRODUCTION

There was a time in my life where I could have told you how to sneak into every single pool at each luxury hotel in Dallas, Texas.

I had become quite efficient at doing so.

Here was my strategy: I wore my swimsuit under my clothes. I told the valet I was going to the spa and walked straight to the elevator. I walked into the pool area behind someone with a key. Instead of charging my guacamole and vodka soda to my room, I told the pool boy I'd just put it on my card. Voila!

Why would I want to go to all this effort to hang out at a hotel pool where I was not a guest? We'll get to that shortly.

On one sunny afternoon, I was journaling, sunbathing, and snacking at a terrace pool in an affluent part of Dallas, known as "Uptown."

This particular day had a bit of magic to it.

Skyscrapers glimmered around me, the pool a glamorous oasis from the August city heat. My guacamole was fresh. The people I watched at this high-end hotel painted a picture of what I knew my life was meant to be.

I was open to limitless possibilities.

I had just finished an incredible session with a life-coaching client. It was work that I loved, but I sensed that a change was upon me. I felt I was on the verge of a new phase of life and business. But I didn't know exactly what that would mean yet.

Two years before, I finished my masters of science in counseling degree. (I had hundreds of thousands of dollars in student loan debt to prove it.)

Three years before, I had moved to Dallas with a beat-up car, a janky phone, and a $625 monthly budget to rent an apartment.

Not long before that, I was living in a dorm after fleeing a religious cult in the middle of the night. Yeah, *seriously*... (But that's a story for my next book.)

To put myself through school, I worked as a nanny for multiple families while cocktail serving and working as a buyer at Buffalo Exchange, while simultaneously taking out student loans just to make it all happen.

By this August day, I had quit my various jobs and finally reached the point of supporting myself with my business. My business was my baby—I pulled many all-nighters studying social media and digital marketing, teaching myself to build my first website, and creating online content. I had even hung flyers at every single Starbucks in my area each day for months upon months. Although it took a few years to learn to get clients, I felt so accomplished that my business was now my full-time job.

I had come a long way. And while I was enjoying the terrace's luxurious environment, I was not actually a guest at the hotel it was attached to.

You see, a five-star resort was certainly not something I would have spent money on at that time.

I would have told you that I "couldn't afford it" —a phrase completely extinct from my vocabulary now, but not for the reasons you might think.

Looking back, it's clear to me that what I believed I could and couldn't afford had little to do with the amount of money in my bank account, the amount of credit card debt I had, the fact that my business was only a few years old (while it was doing well and supporting me—it wasn't *yet* making millions).

More than anything, my ideas about what I could and could not do came from my beliefs about who I was, where I came from, and where I was going.

I was not someone who stayed at hotels like that. That simply did not fit into my ideas of what was possible for me.

And even though I wouldn't have purchased a room at that hotel, I had the good sense to position myself in environments, neighborhoods, schools, and circles that reminded me, educated me, and showed me that wealth was out there—and as I sensed deeply—was made for me.

This brings me to why I snuck into that hotel pool that hot summer day.

I knew I was made for opulent environments, so I had made a habit of putting myself into them. I hadn't yet studied vibration or frequency, which we'll get into later, but I intuitively knew that if I wanted to create a life for myself where the best of the best was standard, I had to practice reaching toward it and becoming comfortable with it.

Slowly, over time, I had been allowing myself to shed the belief systems, logic, and subsequent restrictions I was accustomed to. These paradigms had become a part of my identity via my family, societal ideas, and the culture of the small town in which I was raised. And they kept me conducting myself as someone who couldn't afford and would never have certain things—namely money.

When I came into contact with someone who was either born into or had created financial circumstances that I desired, I paid attention to how they spent money, how they spoke of money, and what they believed about money. More than anything, I allowed their life, career, and bank account to be an indicator of a possibility that was available to me— no matter how far out of reach or vastly different from my current reality their life seemed.

I encourage you to consider this approach as you move through this book. Put aside where you come from, what you've been told is possible for someone like you, your feelings toward those who've had it easier than you, what your family might think, and the notions of limitation as a whole.

Consider the idea that the possibilities for your life, wealth, and abundance are greater than what you've allowed yourself to imagine. Be willing to open your mind, heart, and understanding to a new way of thinking about and conducting yourself with money. *Let the stories in this book be an example of what's possible for you.*

Oh, back to that sunny day on the terrace pool.

While journaling about what was next in my business, who I most wanted to help, what I most wanted to help with and what I had endless interest in.

✱ I wanted to serve as many people as possible and make as big of a difference in their lives as possible. I thought about what would create the biggest transformation in my life. Obvious answer: *Money.*

Money had always felt limited, easier for people who weren't me, and basically, like a big mystery. I was getting the hang of generating more, bit by bit, and was beginning to intentionally "manifest" without really comprehending how it all worked. I knew there was something more, something I wasn't getting, something I yearned to fully understand.

On the cusp of inspiration, I wrote this prayer:

✱ *Teach me how to earn and receive money, and I promise to teach women everywhere to do the same.*

The thing about that prayer was . . . I meant it.

And in the days, weeks, and months, and many years since (and truly for many years before I even knew to pray this prayer), I have been on a journey. A journey of releasing my limiting ideas and perceptions about money and healing my past experience of and relationship with money. I've formed new patterns and dynamics that I operated in concerning money, creating new ways of conducting myself with money that support me and my desires. Simply put, I've become a *Wealthy Woman*, teaching everything I know to hundreds of thousands of women worldwide—fulfilling that promise, the prayer I made by the pool that day.

I live, breathe, and teach this promise. Between my digital courses, training bundles, meditations, YouTube videos, podcast episodes, social media posts, articles for publications such as *Forbes* and *Business Insider,* blogs and email newsletters, I have created thousands upon thousands of pieces of content reflecting my desire and intention to empower women around money. It has become my mission and purpose.

Simply put, *I am here to get money into the hands of good-hearted women who are here to change the world.*

Since you have picked up this book, I believe that's you.

So, hi. I am Amanda Frances.

I am an entrepreneur, business mentor, and thought leader on the subject of financial empowerment for women. I am the sole owner of a multimillion-dollar coaching and online education company with users in ninety-nine countries and clients in eighty-five countries.

And I am here to change your life.

In this book, I combine my background in ministry and mental health counseling, with practical advice and a deep knowledge of spiritual and energetic principles to support you in healing your relationship and past experiences with money and forming an entirely new financial reality and way of being.

I have a sense that my methods and teachings are not quite like any "money coach" or financial expert you've before encountered, but I'll let you be the judge of that.

So, take your time. Take it one page at a time. Consider the concepts. Marinate on the methods. Ponder the possibilities. Play with what I'm presenting here.

Notice what resonates for you, what creates an expansive feeling in you, what irritates the shit out of you, what makes you question everything, and what feels true about life, money, and the world for you deep inside your soul.

Integrate the ways of thinking and being that feel good or right to you into your life as you go.

Note that each chapter builds on the one before it, but feel free to skip something if it doesn't speak to you.

You can read a chapter or a section multiple times if needed. And come back to the book as you need.

When it comes to the journal prompts and homework found at the end of each chapter, consider digging deep into what is going on below the surface for you.

Trust yourself. Trust the process. And believe.

You've got this. I love you. I am so happy you are here.

ONE

....

THE ENERGY OF MONEY

P eople often have trouble saying exactly what their genius is.

I don't.

I am an expert on the energy and frequency of money. I understand deeply how to become an energetic match for money, attract more of it into your life, and completely transform your relationship with it.

And to say it even more clearly: *I understand how money works.*

It's okay if that last sentence made you roll your eyes, shake your head, or say something mean. I don't have to convince you of anything about me. I just have to get you to pay attention long enough to begin to see a few things differently.

What I mean when I say that I get how this whole money thing works is: I get why you have it. Why you don't. And why you can't keep it. I know why your debt comes back after you

1

pay it off. Why you are or are not getting raises. And why an unexpected bill shows up to take away your savings, etc. Because of this, I know how to help you to create an entirely different relationship with money so that you can have an entirely new experience with money.

You do not have to dread opening bills, feel guilty about your debt, experience shame around past financial mistakes, have fear of your money running out, or feel that subtle doubt that says you will never be able to create a financial reality that you feel good about.

It doesn't matter how it has been up until now. It doesn't matter what it was like for your parents, what town you are from, how you were raised, who you know that lost money at some point, who you work for, what industry you are in, or what sad or scary thing you've been taught about people who have money.

These are real factors that have contributed to your current identity and reality, and they will inform some of the inner and outer work you will do around money. However, they certainly do not have the final say in your financial success, future reality, and what you create from here. No matter what barriers, roadblocks, and pit stops are real for you, *what matters most right now is that you are open and available to a new way of seeing, thinking, and believing when it comes to money.*

Because of my relationship with and understanding of money, I became a self-made millionaire at thirty-one and a self-made multimillionaire at thirty-two.

My company's monthly revenue continues to increase month by month and year by year, regardless of the economy, world events, or outside noise and speculations.

Amid a global pandemic, Amanda Frances Incorporated (AFI) has averaged $440,000 cash received each month and hit a record-breaking month of $586,000 in May of 2020. I am on track to generate over $5 million this year (which is up 37 percent from 2019 and 81 percent from 2018).

While I am an entrepreneur who creates online training programs to help people start and grow businesses, I have seen the concepts and principles I am sharing in this book work time and time again for thousands of people across a multitude of backgrounds, industries, and circumstances.

The energy of money is not limited to a job or by a job. Regardless of where you come from or how you currently do or don't receive money, please know that your experience can be expanded, transformed, and completely revolutionized.

Money doesn't care what you look like, where you come from, or how you feel the world should or should not treat you. Money is only responding to your vibration, and your thoughts, feelings, and patterns toward it.

So, how did I get here?

My Background

I am going to take you back to Sand Springs, Oklahoma, where I was born into a lower-middle-class family. We weren't poor, but we certainly weren't rich.

There was a trailer park within a mile of my house. There was a neighborhood of five-bedroom homes one mile the other way.

I have always been fascinated by the concept of money. As a child, I would pay attention to the affluent parents of my "rich friends" and how these adults handled themselves when it came to money. I would take note of what they spent money on, how they talked about money, and the innate worthiness they seemed to feel around money. Their children (my friends) often seemed to take their clothes, toys, and Lunchables for granted.

I didn't. In our house, we made our own version of Lunchables by cutting slices of bologna and Kraft cheddar cheese into squares and sticking these in a reused plastic container with the generic brand equivalent to Ritz crackers.

I remember learning that juice boxes cost a lot more than Kool-Aid, that it was preferred that my sister, mom, and I shared bathwater, and that the unforgivable sin was leaving a light on in a room you weren't in. My mom was known to frequently say, "It all adds up." The electric bill was not something she was willing to fuck with. Fears around money could be felt all day, every day. It was palpable.

That being said, there was always food on the table. My dad was employed at the same company for thirty-seven years. I did not ever worry about going hungry. I had clothes from the consignment shop and Walmart.

I fully and completely know that I had it better, and different, than many other people. I always had some amount of financial privilege. I also have white privilege. This

4

means that I likely had less hurdles than many of our brothers and sisters of color in moving through the world.

I am a White girl born to parents who are still married, who cared about me, and who chose to live in a small and safe town in Oklahoma. My mom cleaned houses and my dad worked as an umpire on evenings and weekends (in addition to his regular job) to make everything work. I honor everything my parents did to create a stable life for me.

I also know that *nothing* about where I come from adds up to the life that I have created.

No one funded my business or education. No one took me under their wing and showed me the way. What I have today is largely a result of my determination to create and maintain an internal state, coupled with external actions that support my decision to grow in my wealth and abundance.

My favorite success stories are the ones where the desired outcome should have been impossible to achieve but occurred anyway. I would put my life into this category.

About five years into my business, I coined the phrase *unrealistic goal achiever* to describe people like myself, as my company's continual and rapid growth and reach was wildly unprecedented. Today, AFI is a multimillion-dollar brand, consistently generating seven-plus figures each quarter.

All of which, I believe, puts me in a good position to write this book.

It is my intention that this book supports you in creating a reliable and enjoyable alliance with money and flips upside-down any thoughts, beliefs, patterns, ways of being, and habits that do not support you in having everything you want.

As a child, I was taught always to spend as little as possible, to cut back everywhere you could, and to embrace an energy of restriction. ← this

The problem is: *restriction can look a lot like responsibility.*

Now, of course, my parents and a lot of other middle-class people did the best they knew how to do when attempting to restrict spending in order to increase savings, or simply to have enough to get by. But by the end of this book, you will know and understand that a lot of "smart" things we are taught to do or not do with money are the very things that keep us stuck in painful financial cycles that feel impossible to break.

You'll also understand that everything has a frequency. And that you can intentionally alter the frequency of a thought or action to have it support you in creating a desired result.

The Energy of Money

When I was a child, observing the parents of my friends who had money, I couldn't help noticing that there was something very different about them. There was a unique energy to those who "didn't have to worry about money" and it felt so distinctly different than what I felt in my home.

Today, I understand and *live in* this energy.

You see, the energy of restriction and lack is fundamentally the opposite of the feeling of freedom and abundance.

Around the dinner table, my parents often talked about people who "had more money than they knew what to do with." The phrase stuck in my mind. I decided a very long time ago to become a person who had more money than she knew what to do with.

The first month that I paid myself, paid my team, paid the balance on my company credit cards, paid the balance on my personal credit cards, set aside the money for bills for the next month, shopped, spent, ate, traveled, donated in all the ways I wanted, and still put $100,000 in my personal savings account for the month . . . I knew I had done it.

And I've done this (and so much more) countless times since.

I grew up in a household drenched in the fear of never having enough money, of ending up homeless somehow, or of falling into financial ruin.

Today, I continually experience overflow.

(When I reference *overflow*, I am simply talking about having money left over. After meeting all financial obligations and all financial desires for a period of time, having money left.)

Today, I own a $3.5 million house at the edge of Beverly Hills and West Hollywood in addition to two investment properties.

Today, I am widely regarded as a thought leader on financial empowerment for women.

Today, money is not ever a reason I say "no" to a desire.

As you'll see, I keep no secrets when it comes to explaining my processes around my financial growth to others.

It is my soul's mission and my life's purpose to empower women to break through all that has held them back so they can actively design a life in which they have whatever they desire when it comes to earning, generating, and receiving money.

This is my very favorite thing to do—and teach—on the planet.

I'm not just good at this work; I am an expert. I don't regurgitate this stuff for fun. I live this work. I embody this work daily. It's why I'm alive.

I work the principles in this book like they are my full-time job. And as you immerse yourself in these teachings, you will find yourself thinking about, relating to, feeling different about, and manifesting more money.

So, let's go.

Now, if you are familiar with the personal development (commonly known as *self-help*) space, you may know that there are a lot of people out proclaiming that money is energy, that getting paid is just an energetic exchange, and reminding you to be as "high vibe" as possible in relation to money. At first glance, it might seem like their work might seem a lot like mine.

While some of these commonly shared teachings are truthful, the vast majority are regurgitated clichés being spouted by people who don't actually know what they mean. In spiritual circles, financial concepts are often shared in ways that lack understanding or depth. There are many layers to our relationship with money. These layers and your level of understanding around them have a lot to do with why you do or don't have money.

In this book, I promise only to share what will revolutionize and transform your relationship with, and experience of, money and not waste your time with nonsense in the process. We will focus only on what will create the most change.

I want to help you create financial transformation as quickly and easily as possible in your life.

In order to do this, there are some things that I need you to know.

Let's get started. This is the first lesson of the first chapter (so pay attention).

Everything Is Energy, Everything *Has* Energy

The energy with which you do a thing determines the outcome of that thing.

 Meaning, the intention, expectation, and emotion in which you do a thing has more to do with the result of that action than you have allowed yourself to realize.

You are able to embody various energies.

The thoughts you think, feelings you feel, words you say, and ways you move all create an energy within you.

- Energy is created through emotions.
- Energy is created through words.
- Energy is created through visualization or imagination.
- Energy is created through holding an intention.

When you choose to think thoughts, feel feelings, say words, and move in ways that bring about a feeling within you, you are now vibrating at that frequency.

As you vibrate at that frequency, you attract from that frequency.

Everything has a frequency.

Money has a frequency.

As you vibrate at a frequency of more money coming to you, the easier you will create more of that reality.

Opportunities for money will come. Unexpected money will come. And you will view the money you do have very differently.

When it comes to the "smart" things we are taught to do with money, no one has told us that choosing not to spend money out of a desire to honor your money and love yourself and choosing not to spend money out of a fear that money is running out puts you into two very different energetic states.

It's not because one is right and one is wrong, or one good and one bad. It's because the thoughts and feelings you experience when making the choice not to spend money can create very different realities.

One of the things I've been a genius at—that I've been experimenting with and learning about for a long time—is embodying the vibration of money.

I know how money feels. I know how to get into the energetic state of receiving money, having money, investing money and expecting more and more money as a default standard of my existence.

(I will go deeper into how money is only responding to your energy—not whether you are good or bad or right or wrong—in the next chapter.)

Before we go on, I need you to know that many of my money beliefs are slightly controversial. I'm not your average financial empowerment educator:

- I don't believe earnings have to drastically fluctuate. Once you are an energetic match for a certain income range, it doesn't have to go up and down thereafter. You can choose for it to stay the same as a default. You can also choose for it to continually go up. (Many entrepreneurs struggle with this.)

- I don't believe we have to choose between spending and saving. I believe in having so much extra (and such deep feelings of worth supporting you) and that there is more than enough to save, spend, and give some away.

- I don't believe debt is bad—it's just a vibration. It is a choice to pay something off over time. But I also know we can eliminate it, realize we are worthy of the things we spent money on, not be a match to it, and no longer be available for it.

- And I believe that there have been times in the past where spending money I technically didn't have, deeply served me.

I will dig deeply into the energies of abundance, wealth, saving, investing, spending, and eliminating debt throughout this book. And I will do everything I can to help you change your financial reality, just as I have for the thousands of women who have enrolled in my digital course around money (shout out to the Money Mentality Makeover Mavens) and for my private clients (many of whom have become millionaires), and as I have done for myself.

Today, I love money. I trust money. I know that how money responds to me is largely determined by how I respond to it. I know that I can create any financial reality I choose.

I know that many dynamics and paradigms for financial abundance (the energy of *more than enough*) exist and many dynamics and paradigms for lack (or the energy of *never enough*) exist as well.

I know that it's all available and I know how to tune into and attract from a state of more than enough.

At the end of each chapter, I will give you writing prompts and/or homework to help you to access and embody the energies that will support you in generating money and building wealth.

These prompts will also assist you in identifying and eliminating thoughts, beliefs, patterns, and feelings that do not support you in receiving what you want.

As a former therapist who has been coaching women for a decade and as a digital course creator who has served thousands of women via her courses and the included homework, I believe deeply in your ability to access a magnitude of wisdom, information, and guidance that lives inside of you through this type of guided inner work.

I encourage you to free write in your journal or on your computer what comes up for you (any and all thoughts, emotions, frustrations, and so forth) with each question until you experience a sense of completion or have nothing else to express, say, and release.

HOMEWORK

Let's get started. It's time to dig in. Get out your journal and free write.

Note: You can answer the following questions as they relate to money, but also in relation to anything else that is on your mind. What is most important here is that you learn to clear space. When we avoid the unpleasant thoughts and ignore the fears that are occurring below the surface of your mind, they tend to get louder in an effort to get our attention. As we learn to look at and process through these things, we make space. We can then use this space, intentionally, to direct our thoughts, emotions, and subsequent energy toward the creation of our desires.

13

- What are you afraid of?
- What stories or memories really bother you?
- What have you not forgiven yourself for?
- What have you not forgiven someone else for?
- Is there anything you feel ashamed about?
- What do you wish you could change?

Underneath that, please write this down and say it aloud with conviction and intention:

I AM READY, OPEN, AND WILLING TO SEE THINGS DIFFERENTLY.

I AM WILLING NOW TO HAVE A SHIFT IN MY PERCEPTION AROUND MY MONEY AND AROUND ANY OTHER AREA IN NEED OF TRANSFORMATION.

I AM AVAILABLE TO SEE PATTERNS, CLOSE DOORS, REARRANGE PARADIGMS, AND ENTER A NEW EXPERIENCE WITH MONEY.

Let's continue:
- How would you like your experience with money to feel moving forward? (Do not worry about it if your desire is seemingly unrealistic.)
- If it were all up to you, what would be occurring in your experience with money?

- If anything were possible, how would you choose that money would automatically work for you?
- If you were designing a new reality, what else would be happening between you and money?

For now, there is nothing you need to do with this information other than to allow your awareness and understanding of your desires, hopes, and fears to increase.

TWO

....

STOP WAITING ON GOD (OR A MAN OR YOUR NEXT CLIENT)

Among spiritual women, there is often an idea that if God wanted you to have something, he would just give it to you. It's almost as to say that if you are a good and loving person for a long enough period of time, you will get some kind of miraculous break and "God" or fate will grant you money.

I have to tell you the truth: *You are more powerful than that.*

Now, I do personally believe in God. I have a relationship with "something greater" that is an important—and very large—part of my life.

I also know this: *God put the power to create inside of us.*

Throughout this book, feel free to substitute any term that works for you for the word *God*. Some people prefer

Source, Life, Light, Love, Infinite Intelligence, Cosmic Forces, and so on. It doesn't matter what you call it, but it is helpful that you make peace with it, stop blaming it, and learn to work with it. (This may involve some additional inner work if you have pain or unprocessed emotions around God or religion. Speaking as a girl from the Bible Belt, working through and healing the religious trauma I have experienced has *deeply served me.*)

We already have the power to rearrange our lives—and our financial realities—within us. We do not have to "wait" on God, marry a rich husband, or sign a new client to pay a big invoice, or for anything else that you might imagine would solve your problems. We also do not have to formally, casually, or in any kind of specific way believe in God. Instead we must activate our godlike, cocreative power.

Now, I live an incredible life.

I own two investment properties in my home state. And like I mentioned in the last chapter, I am currently remodeling a multimillion-dollar home in a very coveted neighborhood in Los Angeles. I own my company. I drive my dream cars (yes, more than one). I have incredible friends. I love my business support team. I'm also in love with a really amazing man.

I've manifested . . . a lot.

And every single day of my life, I look at, and work on, my limiting ideas around what I can do, create, have, and become in this lifetime.

The work has not stopped. I am just more familiar with what the work is.

18

In this chapter, I teach you *that* work.

The reason I gave you the chapter 1 journal prompts that asked you to acknowledge and release the past, get clear on what you wanted, and become very willing to see and do things differently is because YOU ARE IN CHARGE OF HOW LIFE GOES FOR YOU.

Nothing I have is because I am special. And none of this was by accident. I designed this life, day by day, on purpose.

And you, my friend, are very capable of creating your ideal reality too.

Let's be clear: What you choose to create from here is not defined by your past financial mistakes, the amount of debt you have, or the amount of money in your bank account.

From a metaphysical sense, the past is not even real.

It only lives in our bodies and minds.

The past matters only to the point that we decide it does.

It can show us the contrast between the life we have and the life we are meant for. It can teach us, fuel us, motivate us, inspire us and help us identify who we do and don't want to be. But it does not have to define us.

As we work through, process, recategorize, and assign new meaning to our past memories and experiences, we are able to release them.

The past only has the power over you that you give it. Furthermore, those things are wildly insignificant because of this truth: *You are worthy. You are worthy because you are.*

You get to create a beautiful life because you do. There is nothing to prove. There is no one to impress. You are enough. And every aspect of your life gets a hell of a lot easier when you stop doubting, questioning, and beating yourself up and accept that truth.

You are not perfect, but you are innately enough.

You get to choose to be oriented toward growth. You get to choose to better your life and yourself every day. You get to choose to turn around any ways of being that have kept you in patterns that do not serve you.

You get to break the mold, defy the odds, give a middle finger to the doubt that lives inside of you, and design your fucking life.

I get that it might not look possible for you.

There was a time in my life when many people (even the people who loved me very much) would have never expected me to achieve my dreams.

There were many years of my life where if you would have looked at me you wouldn't have seen what was coming. You wouldn't have sensed what I was capable of or felt what was possible for me.

You would have seen a girl looking for the answers outside of herself. You would have seen someone abandoning herself (at one point to dogmatic religion and at another point to a wildly strenuous Ph.D. program she hated) while working multiple jobs, dead-end jobs, and highly underpaid jobs. You would see someone who wasn't achieving greatness in anything she did, and when she did for moments, it was fleeting.

I looked and felt like I'd likely go on to live a possibly mediocre and partially fulfilled life.

But I didn't.

Through this work, I have been either fully transformed, completely removed, or courageous enough to pluck myself out of the situations, lifestyles, and dynamics that did not work for me.

But it all starts with me. As I rearrange my life, expectations, and standards, I rearrange how I think of myself, how life and money works for me, and how people respond to me.

I have learned that you can change anything, by changing the energy you bring to that thing.

By changing the thoughts that you think about that thing, the emotions you feel about that thing, and the power you give to that thing, you can change and rearrange any reality. The paradigms, constructs, and stories around how things go for people like you (which are largely based on how things have gone so far) can change in a moment. You can blow up the energy and dynamics of any situation . . . and start anew.

This can be your moment.

Life Did Not Set Most of Us Up for the Lives We Want to Have

Before we go further, let me say this: I acknowledge that life has not been fair for you. I know your parents did shitty things. I know you didn't always feel love in the ways you needed to. I know you may have felt afraid of being alone, abandoned, going without, failing to fit in, being different, being loud, ending up on the street, or falling short of actualizing your potential and a multitude of other things.

Life, up until now, very likely, has not been fair to you. The circumstances, background, and limitations you had to overcome were real.

But the power they had over you, came *from* you.

You identified with them. *You* subscribed to them. *You* couldn't see beyond them.

That doesn't mean you always had a choice in them happening to you. That doesn't mean that it was okay, or that was your fault. I want to make that *very* clear.

There was always—and will always be—a way to step out of the world, life, energies, and ways of being that you currently feel stuck in. We all get caught in loops and patterns of how things "always" go for us. But we can break those cycles. It's time to move forward in redefining who you are, what you stand for, and how life can now work for you.

We can step into something different now. We *do* have more power than we realize. We *can* determine what happens from here. We *are* in control of what we accept and what we do not accept in life. We *do* determine what we create through our words, our emotions, our energy, our decisions, our choices, and our actions. Of course.

And while the application of these principles can transform anything, I find that for many of us, our financial realities are an area we often become the most stuck. We have believed restricting ideas that perpetuated limiting cycles that created realities that we didn't even mean to choose. It's time to get unstuck.

That is essentially what this book is about.

To become rich as fuck, I had to rearrange a lot of ideas about the town I came from, family I came from, and how things were not set up in favor of people like me.

I witnessed the seemingly very different lives of classmates who had college funds, whose parents paid their bills, whose loved ones were in the position to support their dreams and goals, who felt understood by those around them, and who seemed to have things easier than me . . . while I was putting myself through school, working multiple jobs, taking out student loans, doing continual internal healing work, racking up credit card debt, and figuring shit out on my own.

I had plenty of opportunities to view myself as a lower-middle-class, struggling woman. But I did not allow that to become my identity. I knew I could not continue to see myself that way.

That being said, I had more privilege than others. I am a white woman from the Midwest who was seeking higher education in one of the wealthiest countries in the world. I did not have racial barriers to overcome.

Despite everything that makes me me—the past I had to reconcile, ideas around my identity that did not serve me, and all that appeared to be stacked up against me—I also had choices. These choices—in how I viewed myself, what I began to move toward, and in how I have incrementally upgraded my life over and over again—have made all the difference.

I have become a woman who is willing to make powerful choices.

Activating Your Power

So, how the fuck do you choose to create a new life and new realm of possibility for yourself?

You decide to.

I know that may sound overly simplistic or annoying. Or may make you want to set fire to my book. But there is massive power in your decision.

There is actually nothing greater than your energetic and internal decision.

In order for the kind of mountain-moving decision I am talking about to occur, a couple things need to happen first:

1. You have to decide you are worthy.
2. You have to decide (and believe) that what you want is possible.

This is the part of the book where I must teach you how to change your mind.

I understand that you might not feel worthy. I understand that what you want might not seem possible. I understand that you, like I, have been taught to focus on what is realistic, logical, practical, and visibly possible.

As someone living a beautiful, fully unrealistic-as-fuck life, I feel compelled to tell you that ALL OF *THAT* IS BULLSHIT.

If you want a big, expansive life with big, expansive results, it's time to give up goals that are practical and logical.

It's time to think in a big, expansive way. It's time to make decisions from a big, expansive place.

The logical and practical way of seeing my life, goals, and desires became irrelevant for me a long, long time ago. Frankly, I never wanted a practical or logical level of influence, amount of money, or breadth of impact. I never want a practical or realistic life.

And as you now tell yourself the truth about what you really want and learn how to disregard the fears, lies, and limiting ideas that hold you back and keep you operating from a small place of victimhood, you might find out that you want a bigger life too.

What you choose to have is not up to me. It's my job to make sure that, no matter what kind of life you want, you know how to create it.

How to Bring Anything You Desire into Physical Reality

So, here we go.

Step One: Identify What You Want

I know this might seem confusing. It might appear that there are so many options in life and you simply cannot pick what you actually want.

That is likely untrue.

The truth: You know what you want, and you are afraid to admit it to yourself.

Once you admit it, it is out there.

Once you admit it, you are responsible for it.

Once you admit it, you have to look at why you don't feel worthy of it.

When it comes to life: Your destiny, future, calling, love life, and purpose are way too important to keep lying to yourself.

When it comes to money: Your bank account, financial stability, financial resources, ability to support yourself, ability to generate and regenerate money, and ability to trust yourself with money, and your capability to have money, live out your desires, and do the things that are on your heart are way too important to keep lying to yourself.

When it comes to love: Your happiness, heart, connection, family, intimacy, and orgasm are way too important to keep lying to yourself.

So, my love, the first question you must ask yourself when choosing to activate your cocreative power and intentionally design your life is: *What the fuck do you motherfucking want?*

This is the most important question there is.

That might not seem to be the safest or easiest question to answer.

I have found that a lot of people have a super fucked up relationship with desire. We think, *"OMG. If I just did whatever I wanted my entire life, I would only eat Salt and Vinegar Kettle Potato Chips in front of the TV until I die."*

LIES.

That is not what you want. That is what you may feel inclined to do from time to time on a hard day when you need to veg the fuck out, but that is NOT what you truly, truly want in the depths of your soul.

When I ask you what you want, I'm talking about the deepest desire of your heart.

Now, you might not have a lot of practice looking at the desires of your heart, so I am going to ask you some questions to help.

The fastest way to reach into your soul and reveal the truth of what you *really* want is to ponder these five questions:

- If nothing I wanted were bad or wrong, what would I want?
- If no matter what I did, no one would be mad at me, what would I want?
- If nothing bad would happen no matter what I did, what would I want?
- If no matter what I wanted, it would happen, what would I want?
- If I could fully trust myself to do my part, what would I want?

As you begin to ponder a life of being led by your heartfelt desires, I want to say this to you: *You are not wrong. Your desires are not wrong. There is nothing wrong with you.*

There is nothing wrong with wanting what you want.

Most people won't tell you this, but: *Your heartfelt desires are safe guidance.*

God did not fuck up when he made you or when he gave you your desires.

In my belief system, every desire of my heart was placed in me to live out on this planet. And everything that says I can't have what I want needs to be regarded as a big, fat lie.

Step Two: Notice What Your Limiting Beliefs Say You Can't Have

So, this really great and really uncomfortable thing happens after you identify what you want, your mind is bombarded by all the reasons you can't have it.

The ideas about reality. The ideas about what isn't possible, how you can't handle it, how you aren't worthy of it, etc.

One reason I continue to be able to create the life I want is that I know that anything that says I can't have a genuine desire of my heart needs to be scrutinized. It needs to be interrogated. It needs to be looked at for holes in its story.

I approach this step with this view: Anything that says I can't have what I want is a lie. And it's my job to disprove it.

I often make a list of all the ideas that say I can't have what I want. Then I ask myself, "Is this ultimately true?"

In my Money Mentality Makeover course, I ask it this way: Is this idea about you and what you are able to have written in stone in some sacred land? Did God himself write it on a very holy chalkboard in the sky?

No. It's just an idea. It's just an idea that you are subscribing to. It is not ultimately true, and you are no longer required to think, act, and conduct yourself in line with a lie.

Disproving the Lies

Let's crush some lies.

- **Is it ultimately true that you are bad with money?** No. Your mom told you that and you believed her. You could sit down right now and find evidence to the contrary. If there's not a lot of evidence available, then I fully believe that by the time you get done with this book and begin to trust yourself, trust life, and trust money, more evidence to the contrary will be right around the corner.
- **Is it ultimately true that rich people are greedy?** No. You saw a rich asshole do something shady on the news and got confused. Or you had an experience with someone who had money and lived in fear around losing it and acted super stingy about it. Or you encountered someone who had money and was also unethical. (There are plenty of poor people who are unethical too.) This person may have had money, but it doesn't mean their dynamics for working with, using, and circulating money were occurring at the highest level of giving and receiving available.

  This also has nothing to do with you.

In my vast experience, it has been made clear to me that goodhearted, well-intentioned people do good shit with money. I've studied my behavior.

Money has not "changed me" in any kind of negative way. Money has, however, given me the power and resources to amplify my heart and desires. Having money doesn't just affect how I shop or how I travel. It affects how I give, how I care, how I donate, and how I support. I have been able to be generous as I trust in my ability to have and generate money.

Money allowed me to assist my sister with the funds needed for her divorce. Getting out of that situation was of high service to her life. It also allowed me to donate to the victims of the Malibu fire in 2019, give over six figures to a local youth group, pay the tuition of a medical student in need, and fund a charity drive benefiting at-risk children. It has allowed me to support various organizations, campaigns, and groups doing good work in the world as I go.

Money is a living prayer, an extension of goodwill, love, and force to create the kind of world I want to see.

Money is not bad. Money is power. And we need to get money into the hands of goodhearted people who live with the intention to make a positive difference in the world. As you choose to earn, attract, and receive more money, you will be in charge of how you view it and how you use it.

You can trust yourself to receive and release money based on your passions, desire, and purpose.

- **Is it ultimately true that if you make a lot of money it will all just go to taxes anyway?** No.

Yes, taxes are real. And yes, I pay them. Because of where I live and the tax bracket I am in, I pay a lot of them. Yet, I don't feel powerless in this exchange. I would still 100 percent rather make money and pay more taxes than not make any money and pay no taxes. Having money and the life it gives me is still worth it.

I choose to be grateful to the IRS when that bank transfer goes out. I am thankful for the roads I drive on. I am thankful for the street cleaner, the trash collector, public education, social security, community centers, public health initiatives, and the postman. Taxes pay for those people and services. And while I can find faults in these systems—and easily make arguments for how things could be handled differently or funded in line with my social ethics and values—I am still thankful for them. I am thankful for the opportunity to contribute as I pay my taxes.

Taxes are a part of the game and I would still rather be rich.

I also intend to be smart. As I pay business expenses, purchase properties, and make donations, I continually ask questions and research possible write-offs, exemptions, deductions, and tax credits. But that is because I chose to view myself as a smart woman when it comes to money, not because I have any kind of breeding or got any training around "smart" things to do with money.

I have no need or desire to evade taxes. I am simply grounded in my personal code of ethics in this area. The bottom line is this: The less I owe in taxes, the more money I have available for personal donations, to hire and pay employees well, to expand the reach of my business so I can serve more people, and to enjoy my life.

We will talk more about saving and investing in future chapters, but I hope you are beginning to see that creating wealth starts and ends with you.

- **Is it true that if you make money something bad will happen and it will all go away?** No.

Are there people in this world living in the above reality? Yes.

Did it have to be this way for them? No.

In my experience, people who lost money believed it was possible to lose money. Or they wanted to lose the money. They resented the life, responsibility, commitments, or attachments by which they had received money and they wanted a way out. This, also, has nothing to do with you.

Now, here is something I need you to understand: Money has no mind of its own.

It is only responding to you. Money has no opinion around whether you are good enough, whether you have done enough, whether you have worked hard enough, or whether you are worthy.

Money responds to your thoughts, feelings, and beliefs about it.

- **Is it ultimately true that money is the root of all evil?** No. There are people on this planet who use money to perpetuate evil ideas, attitudes, and behaviors. But let's be clear: Jesus had a treasurer and Mother Teresa flew around on a private jet.

  Like you and me, they required resources to do the work they were meant to do. *A big vision requires big resources.*

- **Is it ultimately true that the only way to make money is by working hard?** No. If hard work actually equaled financial success, teachers and restaurant servers would be the billionaires. As the saying goes: Work smarter, not harder.

  The day I decided that I would take my financial future into my own hands was a very important day for me. I began to shift my focus.

  While my dollar-per-hour amount as a therapist and life coach was higher than the average dollar-per-hour rate and my burgeoning business was doing fine, I realized I would always be financially capped if I continued to only make money through something I was actively doing each day.

  I wanted to help more people and make more money.

I made some important shifts: I began to focus more on the outcome I wanted and less on the process. I began to create programs and courses that could help more people at once (that I could create one time and sell forever). I began to believe that an incredible impact and a wild income was possible.

As a result, I created more influence and money for myself and more success and freedom for others . . . all at once. I rearranged completely how money worked for me.

To be clear, it's not that I don't work hard. (Dear God, I work so hard.) It's that I have shifted my daily focus, so my daily efforts are strategic and intentional. I just stopped spinning my wheels.

As I recently said to my mastermind ladies, "Exhaustion is not the measuring stick for success."

The truth about hard work is this: *Most people don't let themselves ask for or receive more money until they believe they have suffered enough or worked hard enough to be worthy of it.*

Read that again.

- **Is it true that you aren't worthy of money and there is someone out there who is more worthy?** No.

Listen, the people who understand that they have power are the ones who change their financial reality. You cannot get poor enough to help a poor person get rich. You will, however, be in a better position to help others by getting yourself rich (or comfortable, or supported, or whatever you desire).

And I have to ask, why not you?

There is money circulating the planet all the time. It is moving around. It is being spent by people, paid to people, received by people.

Why not you? What if your life, your family, and your longings were enough?

What if you knew that you were actually, internally, completely, and fully . . . *wildly* enough?

I want you to consider that the things you'd like to do with money might be worthy. They might be good enough reasons because you desire them (and like we covered, your desires are safe guidance).

I encourage you to integrate an internal sense of unconditional positive regard toward yourself.

Know you are worthy because you are. Decide your financial reality gets to change. Remember that you are in charge and can break through the barriers in your way. Decide what you want.

By opening to the belief that money can come to you just because it can and because you are worthy, you change everything.

....

Let's continue.

✪ Step Three: Decide How You Want Things to Be for You

Now that you know all the limiting beliefs you've held about money are ultimately big, fat lies, let's decide what's true for you.

All the ideas that have been running your life are essentially options that you never had to operate by but accidentally chose to. This is why you were never dependent on your employer. Or a random blessing, a rich man, or a new client. You simply believed that those were the only ways money could come. Money came in the ways you believed it could—because money will never override your free will.

Remember, money has no mind of its own. You decide that money comes to you. You decide what kind of men or partners come to you. You also decide that clients, raises, promotions, money-making ideas, opportunities, and all sorts of beautiful things you haven't thought of yet show up in your life.

Not necessarily because you say, *"I will receive a ten thousand-dollar promotion at my yearly review,"* but because you make an internal shift. Because you open up to a new idea. You begin to know that you are supported by money. Or that you are being more and more highly regarded and valued at your job. Or that money is coming somehow, you don't know how, but you know it will.

As you believe these things, you show up to life differently. Your expectations, standards, and goals shift.

You create your world actively. (I'll explain more on this as we go.)

Do you get it? Limitless possibilities for new financial realities exist all around you.

With that in mind, what new ways of life (and of money always working out for you) are you ready to opt-in to?

As an entrepreneur, you may begin to decide that the most ideal clients who are ready to pay for your services in full are making their way to you now. You could decide they are finding you, reaching out to you, and signing up with ease.

As a woman slaying the corporate ladder, you could decide that your boss begins to recognize your worth, skill-set, voice, or vision. You could decide that the most perfect people are placed around you for your growth. You could know that you'll know when to leave that workplace, when to ask for a raise, or how to grow with the company in all the ways you desire.

As a single successful woman, who seems to date people who are intimidated by your success or who don't understand your lifestyle, you could begin to believe that you are continually meeting interesting and affluent people. Or always meeting men who love and are inspired by your success. Or any new reality that feels better to you than the one you are currently in.

This is a continual process of incremental growth. Limiting ideas will continue to rise up to challenge the decisions and declarations we have made. We each have our unique barriers and beliefs to move through, but we must stay committed to our desires, increasing our faith in ourselves and the divine, while knowing that we are called to live big fucking lives.

It is time to know that we will succeed despite everything we've been through and regardless of anything in our way.

It is time to become strengthened, secure, and unwavering in who we choose to be, what we know to be true, and in the outcomes we most long for.

It's time to move towards our highest desires, dreams, and callings—accepting nothing less.

The thing is, we are taught that it would be greedy or wrong to want a certain kind of ideal client, romantic partner, employer, etc. This desire means we are ungrateful.

But is it actually wrong? No. It's just a choice. And your choice, when activated with faith, is all there is.

Does it actually mean that you are ungrateful? No. You can be grateful as fuck while you decide you are ready for something else. You have that option.

The options are all available. It's your job to begin to open up to them.

Step Four: Shift Your State

Knowing that unlimited possibilities around money and your financial experience exist, and that money is making its way to you shifts your energetic state. You feel differently. You see things differently. You speak differently. You vibrate differently.

Like we said in chapter 1, everything is energy, and everything has energy. Energy is created by the thoughts we think, the feelings we feel, the images we imagine, and so forth. Therefore, when you feel better about money, you create a new reality with money.

You are responsible for the thoughts you think. You are also responsible for the thoughts you *believe*. Right now, as we've covered, your brain is lying to you (to try to protect you) all of the time and it's creating ways of functioning with money that do not serve you.

Quick Shifts That Equal Big Results

Let's ponder some big energetic shifts you can begin to make now:

- It is possible for you to pay bills in gratitude. (Play with being thankful for the water you drink, the heat that keeps you warm, the car that gets you around, and so on.)
- It is possible for you to feel appreciation for the money you have. If there is some amount of money that you do have, which does regularly come to you and you feel you can count on . . . it's time to feel gratitude for that.
- It is possible to begin to opt-out of the *"It's never enough"* state of mind. It's possible to begin to ponder the idea that there's a reality for you where excess and overflow are standard. (We'll talk more about this soon.)

- It is possible to shift into a state of some type of gratitude, love, joy, excitement, delight, or surprise around money each day. You can choose positive thoughts and feelings around what you do have and what you anticipate is coming.
- It is possible to become a vibrational match for money. You can begin to think, feel, and behave—even journal—as you would if you already had money.
- It is possible to begin to swipe your credit card with an attitude of *"There is more where that came from,"* knowing that money exists in this world and you have now opened up to more coming to you.

Now, I do not want you beating yourself up in this process. There is no need to tell stories that you are fucking this up, not fully getting it, still thinking too many negative thoughts, etc.

Instead, it's time you become what many spiritual teachers in metaphysical books regard as the "gentle observer." It's time to simply notice how you think about money and the feelings in your body these thoughts generate. It's time to notice what you believe about money. It's time to see how you've accidentally blocked yourself with what you believed wasn't possible for you. It's time to begin to know that there was always another way available and now you are in on the truth of how things can be.

Your job is simply this: Notice the unhelpful thoughts and shift into thoughts and feelings that feel better.

Because of the panic, anxiety, and the frantic thinking we have become accustomed to, we forget that we have choices around our thoughts. Our minds are powerful as fuck.

I encourage you to lean in to feel your present emotions authentically, with presence, and to completion without making them mean anything about you and your future. When we do this, the feelings begin to lose their charge and we stop identifying with them. From there, we have a blank slate to create, and the fun begins.

Choosing your thoughts, programming your mind, and focusing your energy intentionally takes practice. Feeling your emotions so you can make space to create and sustain new and more helpful ones may be a new way of doing things for you. But it is beyond worth it. And it only gets easier.

I practice daily.

Every day of my life, I experience some sort of unhelpful thought or feeling about money. Every day, my mind thinks something fearful or doubt-based. I choose not to make these things my truth.

Even though AFI will process 20,000 transactions this year, my brain still says it could all run out. Even though I have hundreds of positive reviews online, I still wonder if an unhappy person could damage me with their words.

Thoughts like these come up, but I know I don't have to believe them. I have a choice.

I choose not to focus on them, play into them, or grow them. (I notice them. I thank them for trying to protect me. I let them pass. I choose thoughts that support me and my desires instead.)

Choosing not to believe them is five hundred million times easier now than it was when I first started to shift my beliefs about my future, my money, and my inevitable success. It gets easier. And easier. As the evidence adds up that it's working, and you develop faith in the process.

Although, I imagine, it may seem like all of this is "easy for me to say," I want to be clear that I was practicing this process way *before* it was easy for me to say.

I practiced these steps when I had little evidence that they were working.

I practiced it when my financial dreams and desires were just an idea in my heart and an inkling in my soul.

I practiced a little every day, and missed plenty of days, and wondered many times whether it was working at all.

But I kept practicing. I kept going.

Over time, the work doesn't feel so much like work. It feels more like maintenance. You go from viewing yourself as someone who money is an obstacle for who is learning how to intentionally attract money, to viewing yourself as someone who money is standard, automatic, and natural for, who simply has financial fears or doubts to work through as they arise.

The shift is this: Money was hard, now money is easy. Money was for them, now money is for all of us. Money was always creating problems, now money is always providing solutions. Money worked out for me sometimes, now money works out for me all of the time. Money seemed complex, now money feels wildly simple. Money felt foreign, now money feels standard and normal.

I am here to help you make these life-altering shifts.

Present day, I practice these steps when it comes to things that have in no way, shape, or form manifested into my physical reality *yet*, that seem impossible, and that make me feel a little bit crazy for even desiring them.

But I understand that this is the work. And I'm willing to do my work.

I know that my thoughts, beliefs, words, actions, and energy are the common denominators for every situation in my life. And that I am in charge of me.

Likewise, you are in charge of you.

There is nothing being held back from you. And if there is, right now would be a good time to decide that you are actually more powerful than that thing.

Because some weird and shitty stuff certainly exists. But you, my love, are greater.

Got it?

Through this work, you will experience shift after shift in what you expect, what you believe, what you know, how you think, what you experience, and what you attract.

Things that used to seem impossible become regular, and then automatic. Having more and more money becomes normal. Less and less effort is required. You know what your job is (knowing how worthy you are, expanding what you believe is possible for you, taking your inspired actions, and allowing the desired results in). And you begin to do this as a way of being, living, thinking, and conducting yourself without trying. It becomes natural. It becomes normal. It gets easy and automatic. You can count on yourself to attract it in, over and over again. It becomes part of your identity.

Eventually, having, receiving, and using money well is simply who you are and how you *be*.

However, this work *is* a process. Especially if it is a whole new way of working with life and thinking of money for you.

It may take some time to integrate. Allow the ideas in this book to permeate and rearrange what you previously believed. Know that the energy of this book is doing its thing and lightening the load as you go. Engage in the process, confront the beliefs, do the work, and know it only gets easier and easier and better and better as you go.

Note: Many of your limiting beliefs may be squashed for good through reading this chapter and subsequent chapters along with doing the provided homework. Some may take a little more time to see differently. That's okay.

Your job is not to make yourself wrong. Your job is to notice and continually shift these thoughts. Here's how: When you notice a thought around money that doesn't feel good simply say, "What if this weren't true?" Followed by, "I wonder what could be truer?"

Then perhaps say to yourself, "I am willing to see this differently. Help me to see this differently." From there, another possibility or way of seeing things may pass through your mind.

I encourage you to look for and try on thoughts that stretch you in what you believe is possible for you, but that aren't so out-there for you that you feel as though you are lying to yourself, trying to trick yourself, or forcing yourself into something that you can't get behind yet.

I believe that your supportive thoughts are far more powerful than the unhelpful ones. Instead of worrying that you are still thinking too small, still believing lies, and that none of this is working for you, please know this: It all adds up. Every single moment of feeling better, feeling powerful, thinking a faith-filled thought, or knowing that you are a creator adds up.

This isn't about positivity for the sake of positivity. This is about knowing how to shift your internal state to create and attract intentionally and on purpose. That doesn't mean you won't ever feel bad, be filled with doubt, or have real human emotions to process.

It simply means you'll know that no situation, circumstance, or present reality has ultimate and internal authority over your life. It means you are still in charge. It means there is always a better way. It means you are wildly capable, deeply worthy, and destined for greatness.

It means you are okay and on your way. It means it's not too late for you. It means, unequivocally, that the best is yet to come for you.

HOMEWORK

Review each of the four steps for stepping into your power and designing a new reality laid out in this chapter.

In your journal, dig into the questions regarding:

- **What do you want?** Including journaling through the five questions to ask when you think you don't know what you want. (See page 25.)

- **What beliefs say you can't have it?** List them all out. Invalidate each one with ideas that feel better and support your dreams and desires as I did in the "Disproving the Lies" section. (See page 27.)

- **How do you want money to work for you?** For your chapter 1 homework assignment, you began to journal on a new possible reality for you. I hope now you can see how that can be created for you. It will be created by you thinking thoughts and feeling feelings, and therefore automatically vibrating at the frequency of someone who already lives in the financial reality he or she desires.

- **What would you be thinking and what would you be feeling if you already had what you wanted?** Write that down now and FEEL it as already real and true for you.

Your job, from here on out, is to learn to shift. Over time, you will be able to shift your state at will.

There are many ways to shift your energetic state.

- Some people shift into a different state by picturing or imagining a new reality.

- Some people shift into a new state by thinking thoughts they would be thinking if they already had what they wanted. (I am this way.)
- Some people shift by having pretend conversations that they may be having if they already had the life they are moving into having.
- Some people shift into a new state from writing journal entries as though they are already living their new reality.
- Some people initiate the shift by moving their bodies. Through dance, exercise, or long walks we can release endorphins, gain perspective, and see things differently—making space to then move into the feelings of the desired reality.
- Some people shift by saturating themselves in the energy of books like this. Or through enrolling in a course or processing with a mentor who has been where they are, or by sharing what they know with someone so they may realize how much they've learned.

It doesn't matter what you do to begin to feel differently. It just matters that you begin to feel/be differently.

The vibe is this: If you already had money, already got the big raise, already had the new incredible client pay, what would you be thinking, feeling, and seeing now? What would you know for sure? What would be true for you? What would you be saying to yourself?

Feel that. Think that. Say that. Do that. Know that. Believe that.

Now you're a vibrational match for that outcome.

- **If you were able to fully step into the identity of your future self—the woman who has completely normalized having money—what would you be feeling now?** Knowing that money has become easy, automatic, and standard for her, what would you believe about yourself, your life and your future?

  What does she know? What does she believe? What is true for her? What would she tell you now?

  Write it out.

THREE

....

THERE IS NO SUCH THING AS A FIXED INCOME

One day about a year ago, I read an Instagram post that, to me, summed up the fundamentally flawed premise by which the masses are being taught about money.

This person, who considers herself to be a financial guru, literally said: *"If you are spending, you aren't saving."*

Ew. Ew. Ew. Ew. Ew. I was appalled.

She was teaching about money from the vibration of restrictions, rules, and by the premise that using money is bad.

Money is meant to be used, enjoyed, utilized, and celebrated.

I opened up my laptop and started writing a passionate newsletter to the humans on my email list.

Midway through, I stopped myself when I realized that I was writing a chapter of my book.

I have been saving these three lessons for you.

Here is why her post pissed me the fuck off.

Fact One: Shaming Yourself or Another into Behaving Differently Doesn't Create Change

Psych 101: Shame doesn't lead to positive, lasting change.

As my favorite psychologist of all time, Carl Rogers, famously says in his book *On Becoming a Person:* "The curious paradox is that when I accept myself just as I am, then I can change."[1]

Now, there is a chance that you can shame yourself into feeling *so* bad and innately wrong that you begin to behave differently for a time.

That is, however, not how I choose to coach, teach, or help people to heal their history, beliefs, past experiences, and relationship with money.

When we operate from shame, we perpetuate a cycle of unworthiness.

And, like we have already covered, you are worthy because you are.

Simply put, self-acceptance is the most effective and loving way to begin creating new patterns, perceptions and a new reality.

It is time we release our guilt and shame around who we are, who we should be and who we have been and own our inherent worthiness.

Fact Two: An Either/Or Vibration Is not the Highest Available Vibration

Like I have mentioned, this is the vibe I want you playing with and feeling into: *limitless possibilities.*

Instead of either/or, you now believe in both/and.

You get to now believe in all the things you want—plus more.

You get to now believe in currently unseen, soon to arrive, and OMG-it's-already-here ways of having all your desires met.

This is something else I'd like you to consider: What if no sacrifice is required?

What if every path that you are on, that feels like a means to an end, had a shortcut available for you?

What if you could have what you wanted right now, or a hell of a lot sooner than you thought.

I am not saying that in the manifesting and creating and receiving of your dreams there won't be work, or decisions, or will power involved. I am saying that *believing bad things must happen in order for good things to be created is not the only option.*

The latter is not a paradigm I personally choose to play in or design my life from.

Once again: Ew.

Fact Three: Forcing Something Does not (at All) Change Your Energetic State

If you pay off all your debt because you believe you are supposed to, but you are so accustomed to having debt that you can't imagine (or become an energetic match for) it being another way—or if you save 10 percent each month because Suze Orman said to, but you don't feel worthy of having savings—you will likely manifest some wild expenses that require you to take out your savings or bring back your debt.

And then you'll say, "Good thing I had those savings," and the vicious cycle will repeat.

What I want you to understand is that whatever you have, in every area of your life, it is largely a result of your vibration. In every area of your financial life, you are a vibrational match for *something*, always.

The amount of savings, debt, investments, and income you have is a result of your vibration.

The level at which you are comfortable spending is also a result of your vibration.

And you are responsible for your vibration. You create your vibration in every moment with your thoughts, words, attitudes, actions, expectations, and imaginations. And it can be easily shifted little by little, as a whole new world is created for you.

Let's create a new and better reality, shall we?

Energetic Minimums and Maximums

We all have energetic rules, standards, and patterns for how life and money work for us. I often refer to these as energetic *setpoints*.

There is an amount of money you can't imagine earning more than. There is an amount of money you can't imagine earning less than.

There is an amount of money we never let our accounts go below (even if that's a negative number) and an amount of money we could never imagine our accounts going above.

Some people can't imagine having a mortgage because they believe in buying everything in cash. There are people who can't imagine being late on their mortgage. Others feel an eviction notice is pretty standard but would not be okay with being evicted. Some people have been evicted and have been in and out of shelters but can't imagine ending up on the street.

And we all have our worth linked up with the above.

I will say it again, you are worthy because you are.

Your financial past and your current money habits have absolutely and completely nothing to do with what you get to choose to do from here.

It's time to forgive yourself. And let it all go.

Remember, the past primarily lives in your mind and in the rehearsing of it to yourself.

Your Energetic Setpoint

Many people have their setpoint, or default money standard, at never having enough, some have it at always having just enough, and a few have it at overflow or always having way more than enough.

You can change your setpoint. You can change the way money has been going for you.

You can change the expectations and patterns that are currently in place.

I am going to share some personal examples with you.

Many years ago, my energetic minimum for earning was $3,000 a month.

This amount of money covered my bills and allowed for a little shopping, traveling, and eating out.

There was a time, before this, when I couldn't even imagine earning $3K a month as a life coach, but as I felt into that number as already being my reality every day, I was able to create it and I received this amount consistently for many months.

I was proud of myself for supporting myself as an entrepreneur. Next, I decided that I was ready to earn over $50,000 a year. I began to feel into and earn around $4,200 a month and got there.

After doing the steps I taught you in chapter 2, I began to feel into what I really wanted at the time: The highly coveted five-figure month.

I thought about what it would be like to earn $10,000 or $12,000 a month. I even went wild and thought about what it would be like to have a $10,000 day in my business. I knew, however, that I didn't actually believe that this was possible for me.

I could, however, get behind $6,000 per month. That was evident from doing the exercises, and I set that level as my new minimum.

I spent some time on the calculator on my phone imagining the different ways the money might come.

I looked at how many clients and at what price points it would take to receive my desire.

I felt that it was already mine each and every day.

And it was working.

New clients were showing up. People were asking for me to create larger, higher-priced coaching packages for them. Ideas were coming to me for new ways to share, price, and package my life-coaching services.

Important: I need you to know that the ways I imagined the money coming in with a calculator were not the ways the money *actually* came through. However, the brainstorming with my calculator allowed me to believe that ways existed and that it would be possible for me to receive more money through my business.

For five months in a row, I earned at least $6,000. Sometimes I even got up to $8,000, which was my energetic maximum at that time. I was so happy to be in the $6K to $8K a month range that I thought I might truly be ready for the five-figure month I *really* wanted.

Then the weirdest thing happened. I was going through the beginning of the month and it was adding up to be the slowest month ever. The way clients, sales, and invoices were coming together, things were not looking good.

What was worse was that I had begun to teach on the topic of money.

Another problem: I was terrified to talk about money. I imagined that people were going to think I was greedy, selfish, money hungry, and in general a very bad person if money was an interest or desire of mine.

Although I had created a training on money and was beginning to share with others what had been working for me, I was so, so, so afraid to share the materials with the public. My fear that I didn't know what I was doing, my shame associated with the topic I wanted to speak about, and the appearance of a slow month added up until I wondered if everything I knew and believed was wrong.

The pressure was on and I was doubting the shit out of myself. Trying to find comfort, I said to myself, *Well, at least I know I can make three thousand dollars a month.*

Here is what happened: The month ended. I had made $1,100.

I doubted myself into the worst month of my career.

One day, I logged into my online banking portal and found the craziest thing: My credit card had been paid off. Apparently, there had been some sort of reversal of fees that equaled $2,000. This also, technically, meant that I had received over $3,000 that month, which was the amount I had allowed myself to decide I was okay with bringing in.

There was also something else going on in my vibration. I had begun to play with the idea of paying off my credit card debt in full.

While the concepts I am teaching you now were developing inside of me, I had way, way less practice with them all. I had never practiced the idea of overflow and I did not understand that I could eliminate debt through earning and receiving excess amounts of money. I still believed that paying off my debt would likely require me to sacrifice in my saving and spending in the style of the Instagram post I mentioned at the beginning of this chapter. (We will discuss debt more in a later chapter.)

Contributing to my internal state was this: I had a long history of piecing together money from various jobs through my teens and early twenties. I didn't have a super strong belief around what it meant or would feel like to consistently earn money through my business. So, I chose to believe that maybe somehow, some way, I could possibly make $3K that month, and maybe someday (somehow) I would figure out how to pay off the debt.

Here is what I need you to understand . . .

There were so many other realities available in this scenario.

I could have continued to believe that between $6,000 and $8,000 was standard for me.

I could have locked in a belief that I would pay off the debt while continuing to earn.

I could have understood that sacrifice was not required.

I could have been someone who believed in receiving a credit on my card while continuing to earn. (Right?!)

I could have admitted to myself that this money stuff that I longed to talk about, and that I was freaking out for wanting to teach on (like, I was writing posts about money and deleting them every day), would soon become my destiny.

But none of that was where I was at.

I was willing to lower my minimum. I was willing to sacrifice. I was willing to be paid through a credit instead of straight cash. I was willing to receive random money from other places when I wanted to bring in money through my business.

I created this situation with my thoughts, beliefs, fears, and vibration.

But even when I was blocking money left and right with my doubts, fears, and limiting beliefs, it still found a way to get my lowest minimum standard to me.

Because God is good. The Universe is good. Money is good.

And all things are trying to work with us all of the time.

Despite the funny way that month went, seeing a credit card be paid off through a fee reversal allowed me to know that I was onto something. I choose to view this situation as proof that I was being supported and that money was always trying to come to me—one way or another—however I would let it.

After that month, I went right back to making $8,000 a month. Two months later, I experienced my first five-figure month, at $10,000. The next month, I made $20,000.

I have doubled and tripled my company's revenue and my income countless times since then, and I have had many, many, many $10K, $20K, and $50K days. I have even had six-figure days.

Bottom line: I didn't let a weird month, full of lessons, slow me down. I used it as tangible proof and reliable evidence that something was on my side and it was all adding up for me.

Now, you may say to yourself, "But, Amanda, you make money teaching on money."

Well, that is kind of true. I also teach on and have created offers on topics such as internet marketing, online branding, digital content creation, business structures, as well as more spiritual and energetic principles than I can count.

It doesn't actually matter what I teach on, what topics my courses cover, my business module, or what my job is. Regardless of how you generate money, there will be opportunities to give up.

I could have given up that month or a million other times on this journey. I could have decided that life, business, and money just don't work for me. I could have settled.

But I didn't.

Nothing Means Anything

I could have allowed that strange month to inform my belief system that none of this was working.

I could have allowed it to mean something about what I get to have or become in the future.

I need you to know and understand this: *Nothing means anything that we don't make it mean.*

I believe in looking at numbers. I believe in being *intimate* with money.

I believe in knowing how much is in my accounts and how much it takes to live, run my company and pay my bills.

And, most importantly, I believe in earning and receiving way more than what is needed.

After years of thinking this way, that is what I experience the vast majority of the time. But when I experience a slower month, a refund request, or a client who is late on a payment, or a digital course launch does not turn out as I had hoped, I do not let it mean anything negative about me or my future.

Meaning, the fact that you didn't get a job or promotion you wanted does not have to mean anything about your future. The fact that you are over drafted in your checking account right now does not have to mean anything about your future. The fact that expenses and bills continue to show up at the worst possible times does not have to mean anything about your future.

These are all patterns. Today we are breaking them.

None of this means that you are doing something wrong or fucking something up.

None of this means that you are bad at manifestation.

None of this means that it's all falling apart.

None of this means that it is all downhill from here.

My brain tried to tell me that my business was falling apart and that it is *"the beginning of the end"* every single month for years. (Which is clearly not the case.)

Do you know what all of this does mean? It means that, over time, you have felt, thought, and believed things that weren't the highest possible reality for you. It means that there is some rearranging to do in how you believe life works for you. It means that there is some discrepancy between what you believed for years and years and what you are beginning to believe now.

It means that there is some lag time occurring as the way new life works for you catches up and rearranges to match your new thoughts and feelings about money. It means that some of the vibrations you held for a long time are still playing out in your life.

But it is truly okay.

It is okay because tomorrow (better yet right now) is a moment in which you can choose your thoughts and feelings. Right now is a good moment to create new beliefs.

Right now is a good moment to realign your internal state to how you would feel if you already had what you want.

And every moment is the perfect moment to keep going.

This is especially true when it seems like all of this is not working.

The "how" is not your responsibility.

At this point, you may be asking: "How? How the fuck will the money come to me?"

As I have famously said for years in my Money Mentality Makeover course, "The *how* is not your responsibility."

Your job, my friend, is to focus on the desire.

You focus on how it would feel to already have it. You focus on removing the limiting beliefs. You focus on becoming a vibrational or energetic match to your desired outcomes.

You remember that there are limitless possibilities and ways for your desires to come to you.

You train yourself to release the "how."

Like I mentioned, for a time whenever I began to desire to generate new amounts of money, I would play with different ideas of how it might happen. I would use my imagination to open myself up to limitless opportunities by pondering potential ways the desire might occur. But I would not view these ways as the *only* possible ways.

Any thought that helps you feel or believe that more money can come to you, is a good thought.

Anything that causes you to feel that a new reality is wildly impossible and could never happen for you, should be examined, thanked, and released.

Now, I have many more stories of people who have experienced financial breakthroughs than I could put in one book, but to help you believe, I will share stories of a few women who wrote to me after taking one of my financial empowerment programs, Money Mentality Makeover.

Alicia's Story

I met Alicia when I was speaking at a women's retreat in Florida. She liked what I had to say and enrolled in Money Mentality Makeover.

As I have everyone do at the start of the course, she set her financial goal.

This is what she wrote to me afterward:

During module one, I realized that I had a lot of unhelpful beliefs holding me back. I was fearful of spending, was clinging onto finances that came in, and felt money couldn't be trusted. I was expecting to only ever be a girl who had just enough to get by. I believed that I had to work really hard and for really long hours exclusively to shift the financial state of my life and was often working myself sick. Within two days of setting my goal, I received an unexpected bonus from my job and an offer on an old car that was sitting in my yard. That was $2,000 unexpected dollars arriving in the span of two days.

To give you more detail, Alicia told me that the day after setting her goal, a man came up to her house, knocked on the door and asked to buy the pickup truck sitting in her backyard. There was no FOR SALE sign on the truck.

The man couldn't have known that Alicia's husband had unexpectedly died a few months before or that she had a young child to feed, clothe, and house on her own. He couldn't have known that Alicia was taking my course and choosing to see things differently when it came to money. He couldn't know that the money he would pay her meant everything to her.

She went on to say:

I've continued to receive more money—inside and outside of my work—including a random $100 bill in the mail!

Listen, money is circulating around us and being exchanged all the time.

Money is always available. But it can't open up to you until you are willing to receive it.

The lesson? *Money is always trying to make its way to you.*

Your free will is powerful. Money will not override your free will.

By believing something is not possible for you, you put up a barrier between you and that thing. Period.

Melissa's Story

Melissa was a web designer who followed my work online. She enrolled in Money Mentality Makeover, and like Alicia, set her financial goal.

She had no idea how the money would come to her.

Here is what she wrote me:

Shortly after enrolling, I walked into a coffee shop and received a $1,000 check, I got three private clients in thirteen days, and had a $5,000 week. It just keeps getting easier.

While visiting her family, she walked into a coffee shop a few towns over. Her old landlord from years before was having lunch. She flagged down Melissa and exclaimed, "I owe you money!" She wrote Melissa a check for $1,000 from a deposit that had not been returned to her.

And like Melissa mentioned, her business blew up. She raised her prices. Clients began approaching her. People were asking to pay her.

The lesson? *People love to pay you.*

I've said it time and time again, but one of the strongest beliefs a business owner can hold is this: *People love to pay me.*

I do not believe in chasing clients, overcoming people's objections, or convincing anyone to pay me or work with me.

People chase me down. People ask how they can work with me. People love to pay me.

I am unavailable for the experience of people begrudgingly paying me for products or services they don't want, while I do work that they don't even feel good about.

Let's eliminate that entire paradigm.

As a business owner, you are someone who has an endless stream of clients. And they all love to pay you.

As an employee, you are someone who has an endless stream of employers knocking down your door. And they all want to give you more money.

Everyone loves to pay you. Everyone loves to give you money.

They are very happy to do so.

Ciara's Story

Ciara doubted whether my work could work for her. As a Black woman, she wasn't sure she could relate to me.

"I'm not blonde, White, or skinny . . . I wonder if this will work for me?" she said when she wrote to me about her experience.

Ciara is not alone in her experience. As a society, we have been bombarded with images in the media that normalize Black and Brown people in poverty. Generational trauma affects how Black and Brown kids grow up and see money. Many people see wealth as a possibility for White people only. How could she expect a White woman to teach principles that resonate with her and apply to her life?

However, she couldn't get me or my program off her mind, so she enrolled. After listening to the content, engaging in the group, and doing the homework, she said this:

> I started to notice little, but special wins. A client hands me $25 in cash and tells me that she "just enjoyed my presence and energy" and felt compelled to give it to me. I am in sales for a high-end product and I had never received cash from a client. Then, I sold $17,117.51—the largest sale I had ever closed at that point—in less than 90 minutes with ease (aka no convincing, no needing to think about it, no comparing to other bids—none of that crap!) This was exactly one month after I joined! I was still on module one! I was like, Holy shit, this works, like it really works?!

Through my years of doing this work, I have seen everything.

I have seen countless raises and promotions.

I have seen hundreds of people receive checks in the mail.

I always say to myself, *"Who even gets or writes checks anymore?"* But those of us who are open to money always being for our good and know it is always on our side and trying to make its way to us, seem often to receive random checks.

Like we have learned, money is always trying to make its way to you. It will often take the path of least resistance. Sometimes that is random, unexpected checks.

I've seen former friends show up out of nowhere to pay back money that was owed.

I've seen clients who disappeared or defaulted on payments, show up to make it right.

Samantha's Story

I will never forget Samantha, who enrolled in Money Mentality Makeover from her phone while living in a shelter with her children.

A couple years after enrolling she told me:

Money Mentality makeover was my anchor while we lived in that shelter. I really got to the root of my belief system around money and abundance in general. I was able to see my reality as a reflection of my inner world. This course anchored me down and lifted me up at the same time. I manifested a job that paid well. I was approved for an apartment literally the day before I needed to move out of the shelter. I received several monetary gifts during this

time. I also manifested my rent being paid for six months!
I would constantly go back to the course if I felt afraid
or unsure. It reset my vibe. *I know now that I am the*
creator of my life. I know that if I desire it . . . I'm meant
for it.

It was only my third year to offer Money Mentality
Makeover when Samantha enrolled. A couple years later,
when she told me the details of her story, I was in awe of the
risk she took while in such a vulnerable position. While I
believe in this work deeply, her story reinforced to me that
this work is not about me or my business—these teachings
come through me to change the lives of those who need it.
I'm still incredibly humbled and inspired by the faith and
tenacity of women like Samantha.

Over and over, I am thankful for this work and those
whom it supports.

Over and over, I see how people's lives are fundamentally
changed through the transformations they experience
around money.

Over and over, I hear from entrepreneurs that people
now chase them down to pay them.

Over and over, I hear from employees that they are now
highly valued in their workplaces and receive unprecedented raises and promotions and have competing companies
fighting for them.

A good friend of mine, who embraces this work, became
the highest paid woman in her very large, very hierarchical

and conventional corporation when she was barely thirty years old.

The lesson? *You don't have to know how it will work. You just have to begin to open up to the idea that it will.*

If you need help, let's return to that classic prayer, *"Help me to see things differently. I am willing to see this differently."*

The reason that I like Alicia, Melissa, Ciara, and Samantha's stories is that none of them knew the "how" of how they would receive more money.

Alicia wasn't trying to sell the truck. Melissa was just grabbing coffee. Ciara was just going about her job. Samantha was trying to create a better life for her children. But in all of their cases, money came more easily.

Each also made money inside of her business or job as well as in wildly unexpected ways.

Buying a Multimillion-Dollar House

Here is an example from my life: Right now, I am renovating my house that I closed on about a year ago.

For quite some time before I bought it, I had over a million dollars in the bank. This was fully and completely an energetic minimum for me, unless I found a house. I felt that the excess money was meant for the down payment on the home that I would live in. (I had purchased a couple of investment properties, but after years of being a bit of a digital nomad, I was ready for a home that was mine.)

There was a point, while I was speaking with mortgage lenders, that it looked like it would take *all* my savings to get the house I wanted. I was not okay with touching my investment accounts and I was not okay with emptying my savings. I understood I would likely spend a large chunk on the down payment, but I wasn't okay with using all of it.

I knew it was fine to take money out of investments, but I really, really did not want to.

I remember saying to myself, *"Investment accounts aside, I really can't imagine having less than three hundred thousand in my savings accounts. That feels like my energetic minimum."* (Interestingly, $300,000 had been my energetic savings minimum a few years before, so I already had an established setpoint there.)

Weeks went by. I negotiated on the selling price. I talked to various mortgage lenders. I did inspections on the house. I got in a big fight with the owners of the house when one of the appraisals came in low after we'd settled on a higher price, resulting in the value of the home being lowered.

During this time, I also paid my personal taxes for the year.

This was, obviously, a multiple six-figure tax payment that came out of one of my savings accounts.

Through this, my mortgage guy continued to find various mortgages with low interest rates and various down payment amounts.

Eventually, we closed on the house.

And a strange, but clearly perfect, thing happened. After I paid my earnest money, made the down payment, paid my taxes, and then paid myself for the month (putting my standard amount of money in savings) ... I had just a little bit over $300,000. And I didn't use money from my investment accounts *at all.*

And, within a year, I had more than double the original amount back in savings, and had a new, higher energetic minimum that is higher than ever before. (I believe in continual expansion. No investment—no matter how "good" or "bad" —is a loss or a setback. Everything is forward motion.)

When you get used to a certain amount of earning, savings, or debt, there is the option to begin to feel that that amount is reliable and standard for you.

You can lock it in as an energetic setpoint.

There is also the option to believe that money is fleeting, unreliable, that everyone is trying to screw you, and that things are not working out for you.

There was certainly an opportunity to believe that buying a $3.5 million house would take my life savings and require emptying my investment accounts.

But I was completely unavailable for that reality.

For many months, there was certainly the opportunity to believe that renovating the house was going to require taking the rest of the money out of what is now in my savings. I was not available for that reality.

I choose—month after month—that the renovations must come out of excess income or overflow.

To be clear, in moments like this, I am still a human who must work through her limiting beliefs.

I am right the fuck up against the edge of what I believe is possible for me.

Which is an uncomfortable place to be. And a place I am not financially in very often anymore.

There is the opportunity to feel that I am in over my head. There is an opportunity to feel wild amounts of pressure. There is an opportunity to believe I will have to empty accounts and move money around in ways that I do not want.

There is the little girl from Sand Springs, Oklahoma, in me who knows she was meant for this life I have now but can barely wrap her head around it being real. So, I do my work. I comfort her. I love her. I recognize when my thoughts and feelings are coming from her fears. And I do what I taught you at the end of chapter 2.

I remind myself: *The money is coming. More is coming. More and more and more is coming. It's here. It's mine. The "how" is not my responsibility.*

Then, I release and trust. (We will get all up into what *trust* means in the next chapter and how to surrender or let go without giving up.)

I also want to say this: While the example above may include larger or smaller dollar amounts than you may regularly play with or think about at this time, the concept applies to any dollar amount.

Like I've explained, there was a time when my energetic minimum was $3,000 a month.

Now, I honestly can't imagine earning less than $400K in a month (and when that happens, it feels like a *very* low month). But along the way I have played with $8K, $11K, $20K, $64K, $78K, $109K, $186K, $250K, $350K. I am currently leaning into what it will be like to have my first million-dollar month. And the work around receiving any of these setpoints largely had to do with what I believed I could have, felt into having, and decided was inevitable for me at the time.

There is truly no such thing as a fixed income.

I have seen teachers come up with business ideas that blew my mind, stay-at-home parents manifesting money through promotions for their partners, ideas for new income streams appear out of seemingly nowhere. Through the years, so many different, wildly unexpected things have happened to allow me and those I work with to reach our energetic minimum for that month, quarter, or year without us quite ever knowing what the "how" will be.

As you've already gathered, this money thing isn't really dependent on hard work, following formulas, restricting your desires, and playing it safe.

Mastering money is about choosing your thoughts and feelings about money intentionally.

The thoughts you think on repeat become your beliefs.

The beliefs you hold determine your energetic expectations.

Your energetic expectations determine how the world works with and responds to you.

How the world works with and responds to you creates the dynamics and paradigms by which you live.

It often feels like fate, luck, good fortune, etc.

But it all started and ended with . . . you.

Stop Fighting Yourself

As you may have gathered, I think you are worthy, powerful, capable, and good enough.

In light of that, I have to tell you something not many people will: *Nothing is wrong with you.*

All the things that you think are "wrong" with you are— more than likely—the very things that make you perfect for who you are meant to be and what you are here on earth to do.

The late, messy, disorganized, loud, intense, anxious, emotional, slightly lazy, absentminded, hot mess that I am has allowed me to be the passionate, innovative, creative, bold as fuck, figure-it-out, openminded, deeply caring, way-out-of-the-box, work-smarter-not-harder, watch-me-do-it-my-way, make-it-happen-now hot mess that I needed to be for my career to become what it has.

I spent my whole early life trying to change things about myself that turned out to be my biggest strengths. But the answer was never to restrict myself, fight myself, or change myself.

The answer was to embrace myself.

And to allow everything about me to be used to my advantage.

Let's be clear: *God did not fuck up when he made us us. Or when he gave us our desires.*

However, we are all human. And we have all created less-than-functional ways of operating in a world that feels unsafe.

As we've learned, the faster you accept yourself, the faster you can change.

And since I am not here to help you attract money haphazardly or sometimes, but here to help you create an entirely new experience with money . . .

This means an entirely new experience with how you relate to yourself is required, too.

It's time to accept that everything about you, your life, and your history is about to be used for your good.

Say this with me: *It is all for my good. It is all in my favor.*

Also, I have fully disregarded the idea that the answer is to buckle down and try harder in careers, educational paths, or romantic relationships that feel like death to our souls while ignoring our heart's true desires.

The path of buckling down and trying harder to do things that felt innately wrong to me actually slowed me down. This is one of the many old-school, middle-class mentalities that I had to release to become rich as fuck and move into having more money than I know what to do with.

The path of going to a good school, getting a good job, and climbing up a ladder is not right for everyone.

And the idea that you find a good job, do good work, and stay with a company until you die is certainly outdated for most of us.

When my formal education began to feel like a slow painful death and when the career path I was on felt drenched with boredom or purposelessness, I took a chance on this idea: *There is something better for me.*

In my early twenties, the religious ideas that I had devoted myself to at a very young age began to feel like a destabilizing and isolating set of rules and restrictions. I was heavily involved in church as I desired to utilize biblical teaching to enrich my life and the lives of others. When I walked away from traditional ministry, I was afraid of losing God, my salvation, and my way of helping others. Paradoxically, I now teach spiritual principles to hundreds of thousands of people.

In my mid-twenties, in the middle of a master of science in counseling program, I found myself bored out of my mind with learning information and taking in concepts at a snail's pace, only to be licensed in one state at the end of the program, when I felt ready to change the world. I knew I was not qualified to work with major mental health issues at that time, but I was confident that I could support young women a few years younger than me in navigating relationships, forming independence, and choosing their college majors, so I started a life coaching business. I was able to make money and help people without dealing with the red tape of insurance or licensure. I was able to coach online and on-the-side while I worked other jobs and continued the deep (and slow) work of my master's program. I was also able to work with coaching clients internationally.

In my late twenties, I finished my master's program and was accepted into my dream doctoral program. When the program proved to be a toxic prison of control, stress, and nonsense, I left it and was able to grow my little life coaching business into the multimillion-dollar empire it is today.

From the beginning, I desired a career that would allow me to help a lot of people and make a lot of money. And here we are.

I've found that the vast majority of the time, a means-to-an-end is not required. There is an alternate path. You just can't see yet.

As I was willing to see things different, I was able to opt-out of the systems and structures I believed were required to create what I desire. I was able to go straight for the desire.

Perhaps you relate. Perhaps you have experienced this in a relationship or job in the past. Perhaps you are dealing with this now.

If the way you've been living, speaking, or operating feels incongruent and out of alignment with who you feel you're meant to be, the life you want to live and the direction you desire to go . . .

It's time to see things differently, do things differently, ask for guidance, and walk away as needed.

I found that I wasn't made to fit inside of a church, university, or private practice.

There is nothing wrong with any of those things, but they weren't where my purpose ultimately lay.

I spent a lot of time ignoring my heart and trying to override my desire.

My life got a lot easier each time I stopped fighting myself.

To paraphrase the Bible, *"Your gifts will make room for you."*[2]

They certainly have for me.

You are perfect the way you are.

Stop beating yourself up. Play to your strengths. Find a way to work your "weaknesses" into your advantages. Choose to see your "flaws" differently. You are fine. You are good enough. You are the way you are on purpose. There is nothing wrong with you.

And, if you can't get it together or don't fit in ... then *good*. This may mean you were born to stand out and make a way for yourself. So, go do that.

I mean it.

Limitless Possibilities

It's only after you begin to open up to limitless possibilities and the idea of things going differently for you, that you notice, are presented with, or find the motivation to go after new opportunities.

Over the years, countless clients of mine on more traditional career paths have been offered new jobs, better jobs, and promotions. Or seen miracles in their partners' jobs. Or had great ideas for new streams of income, businesses, partnerships. It didn't matter if a woman were a teacher or stay-at-home parent—things opened for her once she believed that she could.

Through believing in limitless possibilities, entrepreneurial clients often sense inspired guidance around packaging their services differently, raising their prices, working with different types of clients, or creating new offers that were previously completely outside of their awareness.

Even if they had previously been telling a story about their market being saturated, their pricing being capped or some other lie they accidentally bought into.

Remember: There is no such thing as a fixed income.

The reasons you think that sentence could never apply to you is the main thing that needs to change.

As you lock in new beliefs for how life and money work for you, you will be guided, directed and inspired to do, see, ask, have, and be in a different way than you previously were.

If you stay with this work and keep believing that greater things are possible for you, further steps, new motivation, fresh ideas, smarter ideas, and so forth always come.

(That doesn't mean you wait around. That means you do what you want to do, feel led to do, know to do, would like to do and trust yourself as more steps and actions cross your mind.)

The ways will present themselves. It's your job to pay attention. And act.

I don't like limitations. And I am fully unavailable for them when it comes to money.

But this can't happen for you as long as you are being all "woe is me" and "realistic" about your "fixed income."

I love you, but your thoughts, beliefs, and stories for what you believe is possible for you is keeping you small.

HOMEWORK

Time to dig in again. Pull out your journal and free write on these questions.

- In what areas of your life are you fighting yourself? Making yourself wrong? Forcing yourself to change?
- In what areas are you believing the lie that says you are limited in what you can create? In whom you are? In what you are capable of?
- In what areas are you playing by the rules of what society, your parents, your community, your religion, or your standard of perfection taught you?
- If there was nothing wrong with you, how would that feel? What would that mean? What would you allow yourself to go ahead and receive now?
- If change, growth, and evolution were a natural result of your default way of being, how do you see yourself evolving? How do you see yourself healing? What kind of person will you now naturally grow into?
- If a positive and perfect evolution into becoming a wealthy woman (or whatever you want to be) were inevitable for you, what would you stop worrying about now? What would naturally and automatically begin to shift for you now?
- If you fully believed the *how* was not your responsibility, what would be true about money now?
- If all your unhelpful dynamics and paradigms for how money works for you were already sorted and any unhelpful beliefs completely resolved, how would you

feel now? What would you allow in now? What would you expect to receive now?

Hint: Waiting is not required when it comes to receiving. Continue to use the steps in chapter 2 to release the beliefs and feel into a new reality.

- Is there anything in your life you are partaking in as a means to an end? What is the end result you actually want? Do you truly have to do other things first to have it? I encourage you to ask to be shown and guided down paths with less resistance, where you can receive more of what you want, with more ease.

FOUR

....

WHAT TO DO WHEN IT LOOKS LIKE IT'S NOT WORKING

I have to tell you the truth.

This manifestation stuff is not for the faint of heart. You have to be brave. You have to be bold. And like I've mentioned repeatedly now, you have to be willing to see things differently.

You have to be willing to question what appears to be true for you in order to decide what gets to be true for you.

The inner work is real.

I have been saying for many years now, *"It's not faith until it looks like it won't happen, and you still believe."*

This has been my true-to-life experience. When it looks like it won't happen, and I choose to know and confidently believe anyway . . . magic happens. This is when I activate some serious mountain-moving faith. This is when my will power, my energetic fortitude, and my ability to depend on what I know over what I see, matters most. No matter how things look on the outside, I know what I have activated and locked into on the inside.

How Do You Know When You've Become a Match for Money?

A very common question I get is this: "How do I know when I've done enough?"

Meaning: How do I know that I've locked it in? How do I know when I have successfully done the inner work around attracting the thing I desire?

It might seem like the answer is: When more money shows up in your physical reality. But the completion occurs way before you see it in your world. It is done *before* it manifests on the physical plane. It is done when you decide it is done and know it to be done. That is when it is done inside of you. That is when it is done in the spiritual realm.

For me, I know it is done when I can't even imagine not receiving what I've decided I will.

Now, without knowing it, you have done this before. There are things in your life you can't imagine having or not having. Just like the financial energetic minimums, maximums, and setpoints we talked about in the last chapter, you have this in every area of your life.

You maybe can't imagine not being highly regarded by your partner, loved by your friends, respected at your work, having boundaries with your time, or some other thing that simply just *is* for you.

When something is locked in for you, you might not remember deciding it. Perhaps, it's always been this way for you. Or perhaps you got to a breaking point and decided how things would be and they have been that way ever since.

But you have activated your power when it comes to these standards and now they simply *are*.

It has a feeling of *"that is just the way it is."* It is a default. It is standard. It is known. It is understood.

That is how I would best describe my relationship with money to you: *Money simply is.*

It is stable. It is reliable. It is consistent. It is readily available. It simply *is*.

Because of that . . . I trust it.

I trust money, but really what I am trusting in is me. Because I am the one who set the standards for how money would be for me. And you have too. You have sometimes consciously and sometimes unconsciously decided how money would go for you.

Taking responsibility for that is hard, but ultimately helps you take back your power.

You did not create your financial reality alone. Your family, parents, partners, and experiences helped to create it. And you bought into it. But, as I will keep reminding you until this book is complete and long after, you can change your life.

How It All Works

Let's review what we know.

Now, like I've said, feeling is what matters most when it comes to manifesting.

Feeling equals vibration. Vibration equals how you *be*. How you *be* equals what you attract.

What you attract continually and with less and less effort, becomes more and more standard for you. Eventually, these attractions become almost automatic.

From here—it becomes part of your identity. It becomes your way of being, living, expecting and receiving—without trying. It is embodied.

In this way, receiving, using, having, and making money can become simply how you *be*.

Get it?

Because of this—getting into the feeling is so important.

Four Tips for Feeling the Feelings

Like, I have shared, creating new paradigms with money begins with faith. Faith in yourself. Faith in these principles. Faith in something greater. Faith in the truth that this can all work for you.

I have resisted giving you one certain, definite practice for locking in or choosing what you get to have because I want you to take these principles, make them your own, and create unique processes that work for you.

Like I've said, typically you've done enough when you know you have. You may experience a sense of completion. Maybe you can't imagine it being any other way. From there, your only job is to go back to knowing and feeling what you have decided is the truth for you as doubt or fear comes up.

However, I want to share with you a few things that help me know that I am creating and attracting the thing that I desire, to the point that my doubt decreases, my confidence soars, and I can't imagine not getting what I want.

These are essentially things I do to help me "feel the feelings" (in other words, to help me become an energetic match for what I want).

Tip One: Manifest Through Visualization

Throughout my journey, visualization exercises have never equaled a lot of feeling for me.

Until recently.

One day, I felt led to go into a meditative state (this is simply that state where you are half asleep and half awake, and things are almost dreamlike) and try out visualization a little differently. What resulted was such a real feeling that I already had what I desired, that I knew I had to teach it to you.

Let's try it.

Go ahead and sit or lay comfortably. Close your eyes.

Take several breaths. Breathe in as deeply as you can. Slowly. Fill up your lungs.

Release all of the air out. Slowly. Let it all go.

Do this ten times.

Now, I want you to imagine that you are looking at your phone.

Feel it in your hand.

Now, visualize. If you already had the amount of money you desire, what might you see on your phone?

Maybe you are logging into your mobile banking app and seeing millions of dollars in your various accounts.

Maybe you are seeing notification after notification flash across your screen for payments in your online business.

Maybe you have emails from payments received, client inquiries, or another indication of wealth received.

Maybe you are seeing large direct deposits from your employer.

I want you to see it. Look at it.

Move the phone closer to your face. Move it away.

Scroll through it.

How does it feel when you see these visible and tangible indications of money received?

Notice how it feels.

And feel it big. I want you to go into at least five different emotions you feel as you look at your new reality. Feel each emotion for several seconds.

Maybe you feel abundant. Supported. Excited. Overjoyed. Relieved. Confident. Certain. Appreciated. Taken care of. Or rich.

Feel it.

(If it feels too good to be true, doubtful, or something else not supportive of your desires becoming your reality, use the steps in chapter 2 to disprove and process the unhelpful ideas.)

Tip Two: Manifest Through Speaking

This is the technique I have relied on the most throughout my life. I have found that when I speak or think in line with something I desire, I can get myself into a vibrational state that is a match for this thing.

To do this, I simply start thinking what I would be thinking if I had the thing I wanted. Or saying what I would be saying if I had the thing I wanted. And I allow one thought to lead to the next until I go on a holy-shit-it's-mine type of inspired riff. I often call this *going on a tangent*.

It sounds something like this:

OMG. It worked. It happened. I didn't know how it would work, but it did. I didn't know how it would happen, but now it's mine. OMG. The money came. It showed up. The money showed up. X number of dollars made its way into my life. It was better than I thought it would be. It was more money than I expected it to be. It came easier than expected.

It happened more quickly than I imagined, and it just feels so good. It's here and it feels so good. I trusted and it feels so good. I got what I wanted, and it feels so good. I am so abundant. I am so wildly abundant. I am supported. And this has been proven to me, once again, that everything is working out for me. There is no reason to doubt, worry, or feel confused. It all works out. It always all works out. The money always comes. The invoices were paid. The clients showed up. The promotion happened. There were random checks in the mail continually. Holy cuss words.

I am so loved. I am so supported. I am so worthy of all this money. And it just keeps coming and coming and *coming. More and more and more all day long. There is always more money showing up. In greater amounts than I could have imagined. I am always receiving between $___ and $___ each and every month without fail. I am so loved. I am so supported. I am so wildly compensated. I have the best. I deserve the best. I am the best. I am worthy.*

The point of going on a tangent is to elevate my energetic state to an excited, overjoyed, or confident place and to bring myself into the emotions that I will naturally feel when the desired outcome is achieved in my life. Sometimes, I like to set the timer on my phone for 120 seconds and hold these high-vibrational feelings for that amount of time.

(PS: I fully believe that 120 seconds a day can change your life.)

Tip Three: Manifest Through Journaling

I love moving energy via journaling. (This in itself could be a whole chapter.) While there are one million ways that I manifest through journaling, here are a few of my favorites.

Gratitude + desires lists. Make a gratitude list. Pause and feel gratitude for each thing on it. Feel any other positive feelings associated with each thing. (Such as, you may feel loved while thinking about your partner, joyful while thinking about a new outfit, or supported while thinking about your job.)

From the space of all of the higher vibrational feelings of gratitude, make a list of your desires. As you think of the things you want, notice how amazing it feels to have the things you have. Recognize that more good things are coming to you.

Shift limiting beliefs. Similar to what we did at the end of chapter 2, I often write down what I want, list all the reasons I feel I can't have it, disprove the validity of each thing, and write new beliefs that support my desires.

Written tangents. I like to make lists of everything I am choosing to have in my life to intentionally bring myself into the experience of already having the thing. Different people are able to bring feelings into their bodies in different ways, but for me writing or speaking words is the most effective. As I write down what I desire, from a place of already having it, I am able to become a vibrational match for the place I am choosing to be in the future.

The more often I bring myself into the energetic place I believe I will be in the future, the closer that future state gets to me.

With practice, you will also be able to access the energetic state of the future you and look into what the future you (who already has the things you currently want) wants next for *her* future. You then are able to become a match for what the future-future you desires to call in, more quickly. (This is what people mean when they refer to *collapsing time.*)

Whether journaling, speaking, or meditation helped you get into the feeling of your desired outcome, the idea is this: Feel it to the point of satisfaction. Until it feels done.

Feel it in such a way that when you open your eyes, close your journal or end your tangent, it feels as if it really just happened.

From there, there is nothing left to do—only something left to remember.

Your main job is then only to remember what's yours.

Tip Four: Manifest Through Moving

There is something about moving your physical body that can move some fucking energy. The endorphins flow, the resistance shifts, and you begin to see things differently. I often find that when I move, new inspired ideas come, old restrictive notions flee, and I feel like a whole new human. Let's use this to call in some cash money.

Most of us have had the experience of feeling a bit lighter, more flowy, or more optimistic after a gym session. It is time to use this intentionally and to our (financial) advantage.

I want you to try this: Put on your favorite music to dance to, get on a trampoline, go for a run, hop up on a spin bike, or get naked with yourself and your partner. Once you get into a bit of a flow with your chosen activity: Tune in to the vibration of money.

Maybe sweat is pumping and you're in the zone, and you can literally feel life surge through you. Perhaps you are mid-orgasm, or maybe you are a bit annoyed at this whole movement thing, but you are willing to try it. Regardless, your job is, when you hit that flow state, to feel the money coming in. See the money in the bank. Experience the clients signing up. Celebrate the debt disappearing. Feel the excitement, joy, and relief. Know it has occurred.

(You can check out my Step into Your Greatness—Guided Movement Meditation to support you in this. Details in the Resources section at the end of the book.)

Say to yourself: "*I did it. I did it. I did it. I did it. It's working. It's working. It's working. It's working. It worked way better than I ever thought it could. I got everything I wanted. I am so proud of the way it happened. Thank you. Thank you. Thank you.*"

When It Looks Like It's Not Working

This section will be incredible in helping you to lock in what gets to occur for you. Even so, there may be moments when it looks like nothing is motherfucking happening.

What matters most is what's going on inside of you *before* the money shows up.

Opinions vary greatly in the world of metaphysics around what to do when it looks like manifestation is not happening. Some say to surrender. Some say to put your desire on a vision board and never think about it again. Some say to do ceremonies in various forms.

Here is what has always worked for me: *Come back to the feeling of it already being mine.* Think thoughts, say words, imagine images, and feel feelings of this thing being in my reality. Thank God for it. And then let it go.

Feel it being yours. Feel gratitude that it is yours. And go on with your day.

And when the doubt, fear, or false belief comes up five hours or five minutes later, do it again.

For me, going back to the feelings of what I decided is the main thing that keeps me an energetic match for what I want.

This doesn't have to be forceful. It doesn't have to be fearful. It doesn't have to be filled with "what if I'm not doing this right" thinking. It can be so much simpler than that.

It is just an opportunity to choose a new thought (which creates a new feeling and vibration). It is just an opportunity to remind yourself what you have chosen to receive.

This is my practice: When the thing I want that I do not yet have crosses my mind or when anything related to having or not having that thing crosses my mind: I observe, and I shift. I observe the old fear-based thought and I choose a new freedom-based thought.

Remind yourself of what you've chosen.

Remind yourself of how money now works for you.

Feel the feelings of this already being true for you. And go on.

Waiting vs. Watching

The idea of waiting on a manifestation (or anything else) has never really worked for me. I am a big fan of the saying, "Bow your head but move your feet."

Meaning, while I ask for guidance, I do not stand still. I do not wait for trumpets to sound. I do not wait for God to get out a microphone. I move. I do my part. I do what I know to do. I do what I sense I should do. I do what feels right to me, knowing that more nudges, urges, and inspired ideas will come.

If you are newer at listening to your heart and divine inspiration above all else, let me say: It is time to trust yourself. No matter how you feel you've fucked up before, now is the time to know that you have, in fact, fully and completely been giving everything you need to work with the "something greater" that is out there for designing your entire life.

So, let's say you've been reading this book, you are much clearer about what you want, you have adjusted your limiting beliefs that say you can't have it and you're beginning to get what I mean about vibrating at the same frequency as the thing you want, and it's not motherfucking here yet.

It didn't instantaneously come. (*Gasp!*) And you are pissed, frustrated, or doubtful.

Please consider this: *There is often a period of time in which the things you have previously set into motion with your past thoughts, feelings, and energy are completing in current reality. Don't be discouraged as these sometimes play out and clear out simultaneously as the new vibrations and manifestations you have set into motion also take form.*

Meaning, if you've thought, felt, expected, and imagined shitty things for a long time, you have put out vibrations that are in line with shitty things coming to you. And some of that energy may still play out and in various ways for a time.

Do not let that be something negative. As you choose your new thoughts, feelings, and reality, those things are now at play too. They are making their way to you and will show up in your life more, and more, and more.

You can change things very quickly. Of course, you can. But as you see evidence from your old way of living, being, and thinking—know that everything is reordering for you.

Also please consider this: When the thing you've decided you want is wildly different than the current reality you are living, there are more pieces, components, energy, and people to be reorganized for you to get what you want.

I call all of this the *divine rearranging*. What you have chosen is now occurring. It is making its way to you. The whole world is conspiring with you. Like the poet Rumi said, what you want wants you. What you are experiencing is simply a lag time.

During this lag time, your job is to continue to do your part: You stay a vibrational match through your words, thoughts, and feelings. You come back to your newfound truth continually. You let go (over and over) of the idea that you could fuck it up. You take inspired action by doing the things you feel prompted and led to do deep in your soul. And you do your life.

Here is what I need you to know: You are never waiting on the money to come, the raise to happen, or the client to pay.

You aren't waiting. You are watching. You are watching to:

- See the evidence of things beginning to shift.
- Observe how your inner state continues to create your reality.

- Become aware of what fears are still within that need to shift.
- See what your previous beliefs have created.

You are watching. You are watching your life. You can now see more clearly that what you currently have was created by what you expected, chose and felt worthy of in the past. And you are watching to see how your new creations take form.

Feel the difference? The person *waiting* feels like she has no options, like something has to be rewarded to her and like someone or something else is in control.

The person *watching* knows that she is the observer, the chooser, the shifter, and that she has more power than she realizes, and that she is *in fact* creating her entire reality.

No dynamic, arrangement, or situation can continue without your consent. You are always in the position to take your power back. Remind yourself, "I can always ask, choose, and receive new energy and a new reality."

Also know this: As you live in a new reality with new dynamics, agreements, and paradigms for how you live, this lag time will seem to shorten as what you ask for, and choose, will no longer be so different from your current reality.

Manifestations (or your desires manifesting in physical form) will happen faster and faster.

The Misconception of Surrender

What I hope I helped you to see is this: You don't have to wait for what you want.

You don't have to wait for cosmic permission. You get to decide, act, and create.

There is a common misconception in spiritual circles that we have to wait on divine timing, trumpets from heaven, and signs from the Lord.

Umm . . . no.

That is not what surrender is.

Surrender is searching your heart for the desires that have been placed there and giving into having what you actually want.

Surrender is giving the "something greater" we've been referring to permission to do its part to help you.

You give the permission; it's not the other way around.

However, I have seen countless new business owners give up on their dreams and desires and call it surrender. They are misinformed!

Surrendering is not giving up. *Surrendering is giving in to a deeper truth about who you are and what you choose to have, do, or be.*

There is another aspect to surrendering: using it to make space.

This kind of surrender sounds like this: *This is the way things are right now. They are not perfect, but I accept it as is. I don't fight. I don't fret. I don't freak out. I accept. I trust. I release. All is well. I am okay. I am well.*

Sometimes I'll say to myself, *"It is the way it is right now. There is nothing I could do about this anyway."*

This isn't because there is nothing I need to do or could do about the situation, problem or issue. I know good and well that I could do lots of things about it. This is simply a technique to release control for a moment and move myself into a neutral state.

This is a technique to take my mind, hands, and emotions off the thing for a minute.

When I feel into accepting, releasing, allowing, and trusting, I release control. I take all the pressure off of me. I remember there is something helping me. I relax and choose again.

Accepting *what is* simply is a strategy to neutralize my energy. From there, I can get back to intentionally creating my world.

This or Something Better

It's time for me to share one of my favorite principles on earth with you.

While I am sometimes credited with coining the phrase *This or something better,* I actually have no idea where it originated.

As I had to reframe the concept of surrendering to make it work for me, using *this* little phrase has always done what I think surrender likely was meant to do in the first place.

When you are choosing to manifest or intentionally call something into your reality, I encourage you to be clear and specific. But then, like I said above, you will need to let go of trying to control the outcome.

You'll need to stop thinking of it quite so hard.

You'll need to get neutral for a moment if you start to get freaked out or stuck in your head.

You'll need to do what the classic 38 Special song says and hold on loosely. (Meaning, hold on to what you choose to have but be flexible if it comes through differently than you thought it might.)

So how in the royal cuss word do you do that?

You know this to be true: *It is always this or something better.*

Meaning, it is the thing you are asking for, or something even greater. It's either the thing you've chosen or something so wonderful that you hadn't yet allowed yourself to even imagine could be possible for you yet.

What would happen if you knew that you would receive the thing you wanted or something that was so much better it would knock your socks off, blow your mind, and allow you to see just how powerful your cocreation is?

The Bible says it like this, *"He is who is able to do exceedingly abundantly above all that we ask or think, according to the power that works in us."*[3]

This concept allows me to get into the energy of "surrender" by knowing that this or something better is now occurring.

Say it with me, "I choose to allow the outcome to be exceedingly and abundantly better than what I've decided to have."

The key word here is *decided.*

The infinite intelligence and endless love of all the forces of good in this world are dying to work with you on getting you everything you want.

You have to decide. And no one and nothing else can decide for you.

I decided a long time ago that money would not be the reason I said no to the things I wanted.

And I pay very close attention to what thoughts, ideas, and conversations about money I allow in my space.

My vibration around money is my responsibility. And I view this responsibility and relationship as sacred.

Inspired Action

Like I've said a few times already, I am always willing to do my part. I am always willing to take my inspired actions.

Inspired action feels like this: A nudge. An idea. An ah-ha. An *"Oh, shit, what if I did it this way?"*

This type of inspiration has given me the words to say to someone, the copy to write in an important sales email, and the title for a new offer.

Inspired action has led me to talk to the right guy at the car dealership who was able to find the car I wanted, in the color I wanted (that supposedly did not exist). It has also led me to reach out to the woman whom I sensed had the right skill set and personality to upgrade the technical side of my website when I desired to significantly increase the enrollment numbers for my digital courses.

Inspired action feels like a hopeful possibility, a "wouldn't it be cool if" idea, or sometimes like my heart leaping with excitement. This kind of inspiration doesn't feel like it's coming from my mind, but from somewhere much deeper in my being.

It feels like it's coming from somewhere deep, deep in my gut—in the place I sometimes refer to as my *knower*.

The inspiration doesn't feel forced. It doesn't feel like I have to if I don't want to. It feels like a guiding, a leading, a possibility, a way through.

This is unlike the "conviction" I was taught about in church (the belief was that God would "convict you in your spirit" when you were doing something "sinful" and should be doing something different, that you did not want to do but needed to do, to prove you were "faithful"). This feels more like God reminding me of what I get to do, what I've always wanted to do, what was always available for me, what I was always meant to have.

It feels like a little happy idea, a little nudge forward and an opportunity to make a little movement in the energy, faith, and confidence that I will have what I want.

To help bring it forward I usually close my eyes, put my hand on my heart, and say, "What would you have me do?"

While taking the inspired action certainly doesn't make you worthy (remember you are worthy because you are), it does often bring people the sense that they have now done enough or done their part, bringing them into the belief that they are now in a position to receive.

When I am intentionally creating or calling in something big into my life, I like to do all the things I know to do in the physical realm. When it comes to my business this often means creating the offer, posting about it on social media, sending an email about it to my community, etc. From there,

I ask for guidance and see what I feel led to do, trusting it will be enough.

Grace

Let's talk about grace.

Grace is the thing that fills in the gap.

Grace is when I do my part, take my inspired action, do everything I know to do, and it shouldn't be enough—and then it is anyway.

Grace brings together all of the unseen pieces I couldn't have known I needed.

Grace is the thing that makes it work together when it shouldn't.

Grace is the thing you don't deserve, but it doesn't matter.

Because you are always enough. Because you have decided that you are worthy.

The thing about me is this: I work hard. I don't give up. I take responsibility for my life and my choices.

I do what is required to create what I want. I do everything I know to do. Every day.

But there have been many times when that shouldn't have been enough. The amount of money I was making didn't make sense for the tiny audience I had.

How did it always work? How did I always find enough clients? I always received the amount of money I was an energetic match for (once I understood how money worked) even when my situations shouldn't have been enough to create it.

I can recall two different times when I was $50,000 dollars away from my monthly goal. And on the last day of the month, a brand new potential client, whom I had never spoken to in my life, showed up, did a quick interview, and paid in full for six months. And the price for private mentorship at that time was $50,000 for six months.

To be clear, I didn't need the money to pay for something in particular on either occasion. Nothing bad would have happened if I didn't get it. This goal was simply based on my desire to operate, donate, save, invest, and spend at a higher level. Period.

To me, grace is the ability to have a beautiful, magnificent, extraordinary life while being wildly human and imperfect just because you know, decide, expect, believe, ask, and trust. No matter how much you feel you don't know. No matter how you feel you've fallen short so far.

Grace is the fact that you are beyond good enough deep within you. Because you are.

Grace is the thing that makes everything not quite so fragile. Grace is the reason you don't have to be preoccupied with getting everything just right all of the time. Grace is the substance that fills in that gap as you put your heart and soul into your dreams, goals, and relationships.

This doesn't mean that there are no consequences. It doesn't mean to abandon your sense of right and wrong. It actually means the opposite. It means to trust fully in your sense of what feels right for you and your business while ignoring all shoulds, supposed-tos, and ridiculous rules that you've picked up along the way while asking yourself regularly, "Who says that that's the way things have to be?!"

The Bible says it this way: *"God's grace is sufficient for you. His strength is made perfect for you in your weakness."*[4]

Do the things you long to do. Say what you really have to say (in life and online). Make the move. Trust yourself.

More often than not, there will be room to change your mind, rearrange it all, or do it differently next time, if you so choose.

This is about so much more than how hard you try or how much effort you put out. *Because grace.* And grace is enacted for those who believe in its existence.

So, remember, my love, you are worthy. You are good enough. You are further along than you think. You are doing incredibly well. And everything, everything, everything is adding up for you.

It's all for your good. It's all in your favor. And it's all helping you to create your wildest dreams—financial and otherwise.

HOMEWORK

In light of your financial goals, go through the three exercises I shared with you to help you feel the feeling of your desires having already come to pass.

- **See it.** Do the written meditation I made for you.
- **Speak it.** Go on an inspired rant.
- **Write it.** Try one or more of the journaling exercises I gave you.

- **Move it.** Move your body intuitively, dance to a song you love, workout using the technique I've described, or stretch while intentionally feeling the feelings of any of today's exercises.

Feel the vibration of having the thing. Feel the emotions and sensations of it already being yourself. Feel these feelings in your body and in your inner experience. Let it light you up, excite you, feel you with gratitude, and move you to action.

Go on an inspired rant. Try one or more of the journaling exercises. Go through the written meditation I made for you. Move if you feel led to.

You can do all of this today, or possibly try one exercise each day.

You will know which one feels right to start with. You can try them out in whatever way you want and come back to them in any way you want, at any time you want.

Know it's all falling into place.

Practice feeling the feelings of your desired outcome with greater ease as you go. Practice shifting your state to that of your new reality.

Practice coming back into the feelings, and shifting into states, that support your desired creation.

You've got this.

FIVE

....

CIRCULATING MONEY

At this point in your journey with money, you understand more about the energy of money (and how life actually works) than most people. You understand that you have massive amounts of cocreative, mountain-moving power inside of you. You understand that money is simply responding to you and that you are responsible for creating new experiences and dynamics with money. And you know both theoretically and practically how to become a vibrational match for money so that you can attract more of it into your life.

What you have taken in so far is enough to form a lasting foundation for a freedom- and abundance-based experience with, and relationship to, money. Congratulations!

While your foundation is set, I want to remind you of this: Reprogramming your mind takes time. As you go through this book, and do this work, these beliefs will become more and more solidified. You also have the option to allow thoughts and ideas that don't support you in your creation of abundance to run the show.

What I have taught you can become your new, default way of seeing things. Or you can choose to go back to what you believed before this.

There are many, many paradigms and dynamics around what money is and how it works floating around this world. All of them are true for those who believe in them.

You have an opportunity now to lock in a different sort of reality for yourself; however, other realities will always be available as well.

What you learned from society will be available to be believed. The lack-based approach of your mother will be something you can choose to lock into again. Countless ideas, norms, and doubt-filled perceptions will always be there for you to choose into.

But now you know a better way. So, now you have another option.

Remember that the choice is yours—always yours. You are in charge of your life and you can create a beautiful one. And every moment is a good moment to choose this.

I encourage you to come back to this book and the teachings inside of it regularly—both the foundational teachings and the higher level concepts that we will now get into.

Like I said above, reprogramming your brain takes time. The more you take in content that supports your new way of thinking, believing, and seeing—the more your newfound, powerful inner resolve is strengthened.

Before you know it, your belief in abundance and your certainty around inherent worthiness of it will become your default state.

Now that your foundation is set, I am jazzed to be able to take things a little bit deeper.

It's time we take the foundational principles that I have been sharing throughout this book and allow them to inform how you think of and conduct yourself with money in your day-to-day decisions and experiences.

Moment-to-Moment Shifting

We are all interacting with money all day, every day.

Throughout your day, thoughts about your bills, your accounts, your salary, your pay, your invoices, your clients, and your retirement cross your mind.

For most people, these ideas are linked to stress, fear, doubt, and feelings of not enough.

You know better.

You now know to take any and every thought that doesn't feel good and form a new thought to replace it.

You know that thinking thoughts and feeling feelings aligned with and in support of having more-than-enough are everything.

You know that the feeling that *there just isn't enough* can now be shifted to *there is always more than enough for me.*

You know that *it's not working* can now become *everything is working out for me.*

You know that *I just don't get this money thing* gets to be rearranged to *I am loved, appreciated, and supported by money.*

You don't let the doubt-based, fear-filled thoughts run rampant.

You acknowledge them. You give them a moment to be. And you choose new, more powerful, and more loving thoughts.

Remember, these thoughts create feelings, and those feelings create a vibration, and this vibration equals your point of attraction. Your point of attraction creates your life.

Let's create on purpose.

Changing How You Spend

Besides the thoughts we think, the second most common way we interact with money is through our daily spending.

None of us can avoid spending money. Spending money is required to eat food, wear clothes, pay bills, and get around.

The common middle-class idea is this: The less you spend, the better.

Now, if energy wasn't a thing and the money you had was purely and completely only based on mathematics, this might be true. But we know it goes much deeper than that.

We know that energetic standards are a thing. We know that if you can't energetically support or imagine having more than $1,000 in your bank account then you will manifest a random expense of $500 the second you get $1,500 in the bank.

Once you understand that there is more than just addition and subtraction and dollars and cents at play, you get to think of your relationship with spending (which is simply trading money for something you need or desire) much more creatively.

As you choose to spend money, it's important to look at what energetic state that spending creates within you.

Feel Good About What You Spend

You can swipe your card or hand the cashier your twenty-dollar bill as though spending is bad, money is running out, and you are doing something wrong. Or you can do this instead: Spend as though you are supported, make purchases as though more is available for you, buy things as though you are a wealthy woman.

Spending from the second energy is available regardless of the dollar amount of the purchase or the amount of money you currently have access to.

This is an energy. This is a way of being. This is about how you conduct yourself as you release money.

Listen to me: Spending is simply releasing money.

You are just letting some of your money go.

You are intentionally letting some of your money go in exchange for something you want.

Since nearly everything costs money, it's important that you know how to swipe your card, spend your cash, and transfer your money for goods in a way that feels good to you.

111

The vast majority of the time, I feel good about how I spend money. I feel good about what the releasing of my money gets me, does for me, or how it supports me.

There is no conflict inside me as I spend money. When I notice that a bill, invoice, or expense does not feel right to me, I look at it. Is there another company I could go with here? Is there another package or service that would feel better? Can this expense be eliminated? If the expense cannot be removed, it is my job to energetically get behind it. I need to begin to see it as helpful, necessary, or getting me something I want in some form.

Once again, this is achieved through being the gentle observer of my thoughts and energy. I am continually monitoring what is going on inside of me in relation to money—with the intention to keep my energy clean and my emotional state one of joy, abundance, and gratitude.

From time to time, I do have to spend money on something that doesn't automatically fill me with joy or make me want to do a happy dance, but I have learned to reframe these expenses.

For example, I love paying taxes. I believe that money to be paid is just a reflection of the money that I made. A large tax bill reminds me that I am a boss. Not to mention, I live in a country where teachers, firefighters, and highways are funded by taxes. It is a privilege to pay this bill.

What choice do I have other than to feel good about this? Taxes are a part of life. They must be paid. I am going to feel a lot better and be in an energetic state that supports the receiving of money by releasing the money owed to taxes *with joy*.

Remember: It's your job to feel good about money.

Releasing Money to Have More Money

This is a belief that I have held for many years now: When I release money, it has to be replaced. Letting money go just makes space for that money to come back to me . . . and then some.

I apply this concept to everything from small daily purchases to down payments on cars and homes. When I release money, I expect the money to come back to me somehow, someway, and in a greater portion than what I released.

I understand that this may sound bat-shit crazy and impractical. I understand that it may take a minute of practice to imagine that it is even possible, but (like everything) this is an available reality.

Every single year, hundreds of people try this concept out when purchasing my course, Money Mentality Makeover (you can apply it to another purchase that feels meaningful and intentional to you). They purchase the course believing that it is a significant moment for them. They enroll in the course as a declaration that they are ready for a new experience with money. And over and over and over again, I receive emails and social media messages from people who have subsequently found checks in their mailbox, received promotions and raises, were paid back money owed, had outstanding invoices paid, etc.

They made a purchase believing, and their belief created a miraculous result.

Now, the thing I find fucking fascinating is this: In order for the promotion to be received, the change was already set in motion from your employer. In order to receive the check in the mail the day you make a declaration, the check would have had to have been put in the mail days before. To me, this is an indication that time is not linear and that something much greater is working with us continually. Before you knew you were going to make the decision to be supported by money, the energy was already adding up in this direction for you and by you, and all that is good knew you would choose this and responded in the faith that you would.

Intentional Spending

Since we are going to be spending money anyway, I say we spend intentionally and on purpose.

I say we release money deciding that our purchases and our spending is part of our creating space to receive more.

I say we spend with the intention to form and reinforce a belief that there is always more coming in than going out and that no matter how much we spend more is available for us. (I call this overflow).

I say we spend while knowing that the most positive experiences result in purchases that support our life and our well-being.

For me, spending on purpose changed everything for me.

Let's use purchasing clothes as an example.

Before I became someone who spent money on purpose, I would wander into a random store, make my way to the sale rack, and spend as little money on the most items possible. What did this leave me with? A closet full of low-quality, poorly stitched, disposable-like clothing.

Clothing that would look and feel worn immediately.

Clothing that did not keep me warm in the winter.

Clothing that formed those little balls all over it after one wash.

Clothing that certainly did not inform the world or myself who I was meant to be, where I was going, or who I was becoming.

After becoming someone who spent money on purpose, shopping was immediately different.

Today, I walk into a store knowing what I am looking for. For me, this doesn't necessarily mean a specific item, it means looking for items that feel lasting, substantial, and sustainable. I also choose only to purchase things that I truly love.

I am looking for high-quality, lasting items that I love.

I shop knowing that I choose to be warm, supported, and taken care of.

I shop as a worthy woman. I shop as a deserving woman. I shop as a woman who knows who the fuck she is.

I became someone who would rather have two durable, strong, beautiful sweaters than seventeen thin, frail-looking shirts that would easily form holes and need to be tossed out by the end of the season.

I became someone who feels good about the clothes in her closet and the money she spent on them.

Remember this, my love: Every moment of every day, you are teaching yourself how to think of you. Every action you take and purchase you make informs yourself of who you are and where you are going. To me, this is about your identity. How you think of yourself and treat yourself ultimately determines how the rest of the world thinks of and treats you.

In that way, a $10 sale-rack sweater is simply not just a $10 sale-rack sweater. Of course, there are moments where the item on the sale rack is of high quality and is right for me and I feel excited to buy it at an unexpectedly low price. There are also moments where the low-quality item has a temporary use in my life and purchasing something "cheap" is what makes sense in the moment.

It's not about the price or discount, at all.

What matters is this: The feelings that the item brings about in you, and the feelings you choose as you purchase, and then wear that item.

Now, I want to say, there was a time where I did not have much money at all for clothing. Resale shops like Goodwill, Buffalo Exchange, etc., have all been a part of my life. Regardless of where I purchased or how much I spent, I have practiced the feelings of taking care of and supporting myself through the purchase. *I created the experience of being supported by money when I had very little money.*

This is available all the time.

Once again, this isn't about the dollar amount of the clothing. This is about how you feel when you purchase.

Like everything in this book, this is not something you will get perfect 100 percent of the time. This is something you allow yourself to become increasingly mindful of, knowing that the energy of feeling supported and loved is available, and bringing these feelings into your experience will add up and overflow into your reality.

Large Purchases + Spending Money That You "Don't Have"

There will be a point (okay, many points) in your life where you will need to spend amounts of money you have not been able to or have not allowed yourself to in the past.

And if you are like me, you may feel crazy or doubt yourself a little each time.

In your mind, it might sound a little like this: *Who am I to hire this mentor? Pay this new employee this kind of salary? Lease this vehicle? Purchase this house? Make this investment? Enroll in this digital course? Buy that flight? Make that donation? Or carry a bag like that?*

The old idea is: *You aren't supposed to spend money.* Especially money you "don't have" and especially, especially on things you "don't need."

As we have already disproven: Spending money is not bad.

Spending supports you. Money is meant to be used and spent.

Furthermore, as we have covered, spending and circulating money can 100 percent make space for more money.

The key is this: Spending in such a way that you create a positive and confident expectation and energy with money.

Spending can be a tool for shifting the way you see yourself and changing your energetic state.

Over the years, I have observed many entrepreneurs experience an internal shift when they choose to pay a high level coach or mentor, purchase their first first-class flight or invest in the MacBook they have always dreamed of running their business from.

Per usual, it wasn't the coach, the airplane, or the computer that was the magic. It was their decision to conduct themselves from a different state, viewing themselves as an abundant business owner and wealthy human.

Many of them made those purchases on a credit card—spending money that they didn't technically have. While I don't recommend maxing out your credit card on items with no significance to you, I do believe that spending intentionally from a state of gratitude and joy, while declaring what this purchase means about you and your future, is a vibrationally positive decision. Even if it means using a credit card, a loan, or some savings.

Here is why this works: When we are gripping, clinging, and controlling with money while worrying about money running out, we tend to cut off the flow of money.

As we begin to live from a place of using, working with, leveraging, and spending money while knowing that more is coming and we are supported, we tend to expand the flow of money in our lives.

Over time we become comfortable receiving, releasing, spending, having, and saving larger and larger amounts of money.

To me, spending more while receiving more, saving more, and investing more has always been the goal. For me, it's not just about hoarding money away. I want to use and enjoy money at a high level too.

While I do love, love, love having money in savings and investments, I want my home, closet, garage, and giving to reflect my abundance as well. I want to receive more and spend more. And I want to do so intentionally, unapolo-getically, and with a deep trust in myself and in how money works for me.

Examples of spending well are:

- Intentional shopping.
- Spending that honors your needs and desires.
- Spending aligned with your next-level self.
- Spending to support your life goals and business endeavors.
- Investing in a coaching program or the services of a paid mentor who lives and works in a way that is in line with you and your desired future.

AMANDA FRANCES

Underlying principles are that:

- Circulating money makes space for more money because you are in flow and are not fearful with money. You know more is always coming so you can choose to spend and receive freely.
- Spending (or taking any action) as someone at your next level helps to elevate you to that level. You begin to embody the future version of you and move into your next level more quickly.

I get that these concepts may be different than what you are used to, and that integrating them may take a little practice. But now that you understand the energy of money you can see why they are true.

Side note: There is a lie that is told in certain spaces that you are not allowed to charge a certain amount of money for a product or service until you have spent that amount of money on a similar product or service.

This is not true. There was a time when the price of my coaching was significantly more than I had ever spent on coaching. Not for any reason other than there wasn't a coach I wanted to work with who charged more than that.

Now, I have spent significantly more on coaching than I have ever charged. This is because there was a coach I wanted to work with who happened to charge a high price point. When pricing your services, you do not have to spend a certain amount of money to be worthy of charging the amount that is aligned for you. People who say that you must spend a certain amount of money (by hiring them) so that you can raise your prices, are lying to you. They may mean well, but in my opinion they are using very shallow sales tactics.

Spend money in ways that feel good to you, not to be worthy of something. Spend because the coach, product, service, or price point feels good to you.

Remember, you are worthy because you are.

You can use hiring a coach to elevate your energy, but you do not have to do anything that does not feel good to you. I personally believe that you should stay far, far away from any coach, teacher, or self-appointed guru who tells you that working with them is the "only way" to achieve something or that if you don't work with them you will be doomed in some way.

Your Job, as Always, Is This

Follow your heart. Trust yourself. Choose what you get to have.

When you feel inspired to spend on something that freaks you out, set an intention about a desired outcome regarding that purchase. Decide what it means for you and what now gets to occur because of this intentional investment.

Also, remember that you are in a relationship with money. You aren't sorting out your money stuff "once and for all," you are always building and maintaining a relationship so that it can be more functional and supportive of you forever.

This is not something you do once, this is something you develop over time. This is a relationship that you are in.

I know this to be true: In my life and business, I have many times experienced spending money as a means to making money.

Spending money is a vibrational tool I use.

HOMEWORK

Time to dig in. Free write in your journal on the following questions.

- What continual purchases, bills, or payments are happening in your life that do not feel good to you? Look at this. Maybe it's time to eliminate or change this expense. If it is required, your work is to change your view of this, experiencing joy for what it provides you.

- What purchasing habits do you have that do not feel good to you?

  Maybe you purchase items you don't even like because they are on sale, creating a pattern of spending on low-quality items that don't bring about a positive internal experience for you.

  Maybe your relationship with discounts, sales, or coupons puts you in a state of feeling lack and can be shifted from an energy of *"I will never have abundance"* to a mindset of *"I am so thankful to be supported by these special prices."*

  Maybe you continually purchase things with an underlying feeling of guilt, lack, or fear as you swipe your card.

- Is there something that you desire to purchase that you don't believe is possible for you to have?

Whether it's a coach, program, handbag, home, or car, your work now is to remember what is actually possible for you.

Use the exercises in chapter 4 to bring the vibration of having this thing into your body. Feel the feelings of it being yours. Imagine, see, and feel it until you experience a sense of completion or satisfaction in your mind and body.

Remember, nothing is impossible for you. You can have it all. The entire world begins to rearrange to get you what you want, once you become an energetic match for that thing. No matter who you are or where you came from your desires were given to you by God. They are your birthright.

- What kind of woman do you want to be when it comes to spending money? How do you spend? What do you spend on? How does it feel to spend on these things?

  Here is where we lock in your next-level self and next-level life when it comes to the releasing of money.

- How do you want the flow of money to work for you? How do you want the circulation of money to work for you? What do you want to automatically happen as you release money?

  Here is where I want you to play with the idea of money replacing or replenishing itself easily. If money acted however you told it to act, what would happen when you released money? How would it feel if this were already true for you?

SIX

....

GET COMFORTABLE WITH
THE CASH MONEY

A lot of people who teach on money or manifestation are broke.

I know this because they often enroll in my courses or hire me for coaching.

I've seen this many, many times: A person becomes more and more confident about their ability to receive money, but they do not know to also practice embodying the energy of having money.

They will have a successful product launch, a large month, or receive a big bonus, allowing them to buy some really nice things or pay the bills and debt they've been avoiding. Then, all the money is gone.

This is how a feast-or-famine cycle is created.

For business owners in the personal development or coaching space, this can especially be an issue. They feel they need to share about their success to sell whatever they are promoting.

They are selling their success, but they don't have any money. So, they are internally conflicted and feel like a fraud.

They are teaching about business, money, or manifestation and they are secretly broke most of the time. This is why there is a distinction between receiving money and having money.

Thankfully, we can learn to embody the energy of consistent, reliable, and dependable money.

Having Money vs. Making Money

Allowing the money in is one thing. Being comfortable with the money sticking around is another.

The purpose of this section is not to dig into the ethics of broke business coaches who intentionally paint a picture to present a false representation of their success.

I have no desire to shame anyone's financial experience. But I have to tell you why it happens.

It is okay if, up until now, you have spent everything you've made.

It's okay if, at this point in time, you have patterns around money that don't serve you.

While I am an advocate for being honest online, I know that our relationships with money are often multifaceted and layered as fuck.

And my intention here is to look at the reasons why so many people who learn to receive money, never seem to have any money.

Society would tell us that these people are irresponsible, can't manage money, and are overall bad with money. I disagree.

The actual problem usually lies in one of these areas:

- They don't feel worthy of money.
- They don't actually want the money.
- They believe something bad will happen if they allow themselves to keep some of the money. (Like they'll have to give it to a needy family member, or the tax man will take it away.)
- They can't actually imagine experiencing a reality where any money is left over.
- They either can't imagine, or do not feel good enough for extra, excess, or surplus funds.

In short, they are unfamiliar with the energy and experience of "more than I know what to do with" or more than enough. Their energetic setpoint is tuned to "not enough."

It doesn't matter how much money you earn or receive if you are a vibrational match for using all of it and having nothing left.

Once again, this is about your energy and expectation.

Shifting Out of "Never Enough"

And, to tell you the truth, I've been there.

My relationship with, and confidence in, my ability to have money and use it well has matured over time.

As I have said, you are in a relationship with money. *This is a growing, living, breathing, and evolving relationship.*

For years, I made a lot of money and spent everything I made. I also had debt—both credit card and student loan debt.

Was this a bad thing? No. Not really.

Since I was clear within myself and with my audience that fully paying off my debt simply wasn't a priority to me at that moment, there wasn't a conflict for me.

I made my payments. (I have never been someone who entertained the idea of not making at least my minimum payments and I usually paid much more than that.) I lived my life. I didn't make debt mean anything about me or my financial future.

Then one day everything changed.

Saving the Cash Money

I was sitting in a Balinese airport talking to a good friend who took pride in the extra money she seemed to always have. She said something to me that changed my perspective in a single moment. "It's so hot to have a fat bank account."

Oh! I said to myself. *This changes everything.*

For years, the connotation I had made with saving money was one drenched with boredom, responsibility, annoyance, and obedience.

Savings had yet to feel fun, hot, or desirable. But for the first time, I wanted to create something different when it came to my "left over" money. I was suddenly unavailable for spending every bit of the money I was making. Having no money in the bank while carrying a Chanel bag was just not going to do it for me anymore.

This was when I first started to play with the idea of what I call *overflow*—or *more than enough*. I began to ponder this: What if, no matter how much I spent, there was always money left over?

What if excess and extra were standard instead of just enough or not quite enough?

I began to use what I have taught you in this book ... I felt the feelings of and strengthened my belief in: Surplus. Overflow. Extra. More than I know what to do with.

Within a couple of months, I paid off a big chunk of debt.

Within the year, all my credit card debt was paid off. I have kept these cards paid off in the three-plus years since. (I use credit cards; I just pay them off in full each month.)

I began to make much larger student loan payments with pride and joy.

I went from being someone who could make money to being someone who could save, be with, and HAVE money.

What I want you to know is this—I didn't try to spend less. I didn't decide to earn significantly more. I made an energetic shift internally.

While I continually increased the revenue goals for my company and that increase contributed to being able to pay down debt and save more cash, what I want you to understand is this: I did not create some rules or structures that said that I had to make X amount to be able to pay off X debt and to be able to save X extra money or else I fail and none of this money stuff works for me.

I just decided that "more than enough" was simply my vibe.

This was a huge moment in my financial evolution.

This was the moment I began to embody the *Wealthy Woman*.

I started allowing myself to be really, really comfortable with having money. I began to put more and more in my savings accounts. I got to where I couldn't even imagine not having thousands, then tens of thousands, then hundreds of thousands, then over a million dollars available between my savings and investment accounts.

Debt was naturally eliminated as an extension of the overflow. (We will talk more about this in my next chapter.)

To become the Wealthy Woman, you have to become increasingly comfortable with the cash money. Having money. Saving money. Spending money. Investing money. Etc.

Who is the Wealthy Woman, you might ask?

The Wealthy Woman is calm, certain, sure, and centered about money. She knows herself, loves herself, and trusts herself with money. She only sees endless possibilities. She's not worried about money because she knows how money works and she knows how to generate more. She is the evolved version of each of us. She is the financial destiny we are each meant for, embodied.

For me, and many of my private clients, the phases of building wealth go something like this.

1. **Earn.** Allow money in. Learn to receive, make, and earn more money.

2. **Save.** Become comfortable having money. Allowing access and overflow to create savings and eliminate debt.

3. **Invest.** Begin to invest. Buy real estate. Invest in the stock market or other businesses. Become more intentional with retirement funds and other long-term investment vehicles.

But it all starts with consistent cash flow. Or the vibration of receiving money.

Consistent Cash Flow

By learning to embody the Wealthy Woman, I became a master of consistent cash flow in my business.

Meaning, no matter what I launch, how often I launch, or the price point of the things I launch, once my company hits a new range of income, we tend to stay in that range until we elevate into our next range.

In the online education world, it's extremely common to have a really big month due to the successful launch of a course followed by a series of way smaller months.

I decided years ago that that wasn't the life or business I wanted. I want to have wildly profitable months continually, no matter what I do or don't sell.

There are months when I feel led to create and sell a lower-priced product.

Other months, a digital product that is medium-priced is on my heart to promote.

And, contrary to what you might think, there are actually more people enrolling in the higher-cost offers than the lower-cost offers.

However, making lower-cost programs available to people is important to me.

It's also important to me to create a fuck-ton of free content.

I decided in the very beginning of my business that I would always create free, inspiring content for the masses. I want my success and the resources it provides to put me in the position to deliver free and accessible content to millions of people who are positively affected by what I share, even those who may never pay me.

What I couldn't have known all those years ago, was that by supporting people via my free inspirational content—like Facebook and Instagram posts, YouTube videos, podcasts, vlogs and blogs, and livestreams—it would make it a lot easier for them to feel comfortable buying from me.

I want to help people at every level and every point in their financial journey.

The vast majority of the time, I have more people enrolling at the $1,000–$2,000 price point than I do at the $97–$297 price point.

But I do not launch something at the $1,000-plus price point every month.

Some months I release only lower-cost things. Some months I release medium-cost things. I hardly ever promote my "high-ticket" offers. (These are mentorship programs that cost $10,000 or more.)

RICH AS F*CK

I follow the guidance of my inner knowing around what to sell monthly.

As the payment plans from various programs sold in other months contribute to revenue received in the current month, and as I sell what's on my heart to sell, it somehow always comes together to equal at least my energetic minimum.

Because of my energetic set point, it tends to result in my company generating around the same amount of money every single month. (People usually stay in one range—no matter how wide or narrow—until they elevate into a new range.)

I also don't plan my year. Aside from one or two launches that happen at the same time every year, I no longer crunch numbers to figure out if my goals are possible.

My goals are possible because I decide they are. They happen because I see them as not just possible, but as highly likely, probable, and expected.

And while crunching numbers and making plans can help you to see how your revenue goal is possible and to become aware of various scenarios where these goals occur for you, I need you to understand why this actually works and how it actually helps you.

Once you see the calculator or spreadsheet say it's possible, you choose to believe.

But you could have just chosen to believe regardless of what anyone or anything says.

The power was always in you and your belief.

I may set a goal for how many people will end up in an offer or a goal around how much an offer might make once all the payment plans have been paid. However, I do not make a launch going well or not well mean anything about what I will ultimately have or how things will add up for the month, quarter, or year.

I take my inspired actions. (Meaning, I allow myself to be led by my desires and trust that I am always being guided to create, do, or sell the right thing.)

I believe my desires will not lead me astray. And they don't.

I believe that my company's revenue doesn't have to go up and down drastically. And it doesn't.

And when I do have a weird month, I don't let it mean anything about me or what I get to do, be, and have in life. I look at what in my beliefs, thoughts, and energy created what occurred and I keep going.

I do not analyze. I do not beat myself up. I do not freak out. I look at what might need to be adjusted inside my beliefs, energy, and expectations. And I go back to assuming the best is occurring for myself and my life.

Like I've said: Everything occurring in your financial reality is just letting you know how you've been vibrating. You know this because you know that you create vibration by what you think and feel. And that what you think and feel determines what you know and believe. And that all of this continually adds up and works together for you. And that you are very capable of creating any-fucking-thing you desire.

Sidenote: I have to say, there is a big difference, energetically, between doing something you don't really want to do because you think it will make money and doing something you really want to do while knowing that you are worthy and choosing that it gets to make money.

Without fail, I make more money when I do what I want to do while knowing that somehow, someway the money I am an energetic match for will come.

Making Massive Money Is No Big Deal to Elevate Your Income

The key for elevating into a new income range is making the new amount of money no big deal for you. Once I feel the frequency of a new level of receiving—I tend to hit it over and over—as I make it the default standard for me. I begin to see that amount of money as low, standard, normal, and truly not that big of a deal at all.

I learned this concept from my good friend, and former mentor Katrina Ruth.

I jumped on the phone with Kat late one night in early 2017 to confide in her about a wild fear I had developed. I was convinced that I was going to get cancer—or another horrible disease—out of nowhere and die.

I had also just had my first six-figure month, followed by five back-to-back $100K months.

Kat immediately sensed what was going on.

"You need to see one hundred thousand-dollar months as no big deal," she said.

"Excuse me? Kat! That is like *a lot* of money," I replied.

"Amanda, to a truly wealthy person, they couldn't live on such an absurdly low amount of money. I know that I certainly couldn't," she said.

"Okay, but what does this have to do with being afraid I will get cancer and die?" I asked.

"Your life gets to be this good. It gets to be this good and it's only going to get better," she said to me. "The better it gets, the better it gets."

Kat was right. I was freaking out and creating phobias and fears because my life had gotten really good.

I had significantly up-leveled my life within the five months before.

After coming back to the United States after six months of living nomadically and running my business from abroad, I leased an AMG Mercedes Convertible. (I was able to pay upfront for the entire lease via cash money I had set aside using my dedication to overflow and savings I'd developed the summer before.)

I drove said convertible to Santa Barbara, California, with the hunch I might stay awhile.

Once I arrived, I had my first quarter-of-a-million-dollar launch and six-figure month. Then, through my belief in consistent income, I continued to earn six figures each and every month.

I had rented a beautiful little downstairs apartment in Montecito with a Zen Garden and orange tree that was walking distance to the beach.

After years of being somewhat of a workaholic and months of traveling internationally alone, I was tired.

The mountains of Montecito were nourishing me. The friends I had made there were wildly good-hearted humans. My business was thriving. I was working less and earning more. I was releasing stress and stories at a rapid pace.

I was peaceful. And happy. And my life was really good. But I was afraid that it could all end and all run out. I was afraid that something horrible could happen to me and I would lose it all.

And I knew I needed to continue to up-level my receiving and savings if I wanted to be someone who could afford a down payment on the type of house I wanted in my desired area in California. (It's real out here, lol)

After Kat, in her harsh, yet loving and intuitive way, bluntly told me that $100,000 months were nothing, I had a $180,000 month two months later. And a $250,000 month a few months after that. And a $350,000 month one year after that. Over the past year, I have stabilized $400,000-plus cash months as my minimum standard. As I've stated, my company's biggest month to date is $586,000.

I am currently (literally as I write) working on viewing $1,000,000 months as no big deal because I understand that this is the only way to get my very human brain to be able to receive these insane amounts of money continually.

What the Fuck Do I Even Do with That Much Money

It is very understandable to wonder what someone does with such large amounts of money.

To be honest, as you make more money, nothing really changes. And everything changes.

You don't worry about bills anymore. You don't worry about buying what you need, paying something off, or helping someone with something. (The choice to worry is always available, but I've gotten more and more used to simply not going to that place.)

Money flows and you expect it to. But you're still basically the same person. You just have more resources. Resources that make it easier to do what you feel called to do.

And everything begins to expand.

Amanda Frances Inc. is able to pay a team of people for doing their great work. We have customer support people, a graphic designer, a social media manager, a video editor, a publicist, an attorney, and an accountant. As I hire others to help me, my time and energy expand. I can focus on the things that only I can do such as holding the vision, running the company, teaching the trainings, etc.

Team AF is able to sustain itself as we support the tens of thousands of people enrolled in paid offers and the hundreds of thousands of people who consume my free, inspirational, empowering content.

I am supported in getting my work out into the world. I am supported through the home I live in, the cars I drive, the clothes I wear, and the places I travel.

I am able to give and donate freely when I am moved by a cause or organization.

There Is Always More to Do with Money

Graduates of Money Mentality Makeover often share stories with me about putting their children in better schools, living in more desirable neighborhoods, driving more reliable cars, and experiencing an overall more enjoyable experience of life.

The feedback is this: As you experience more financial safety, consistency, and joy in your life, you are in a position to make more of a positive impact for others.

When you live from a state of "not enough" you are financially capped in what you are able to do to help others.

As Wayne Dyer said, *"You can't get poor enough to help the poor become prosperous."*[5] I can do a lot more for others as a well-resourced person. I am still just me. But I am a version of me with the means to make the difference I desire to make more easily.

Money allows me to be me, but in an amplified way. Money allows me to live a bigger life and make a bigger difference.

No matter what anyone tells you, it takes money to do great work in the world. Because things—clothes, staff, schools, food, housing, childcare—all cost money.

Money allows me to be me, but in an amplified way. Money allows me to live a bigger life and make a bigger difference.

No matter what anyone tells you, it takes money to do great work in the world. Because things—clothes, staff, schools, food, housing, childcare—all cost money.

And When All of That Is Covered, You Can Get Creative

Money is not bad. It's required.

And you are worthy of the amount you decide to be worthy of. You will receive/earn and save/keep the amount of it that you can mentally, energetically, and emotionally get behind.

There is no rock-like tablet in the sky where God predetermined, wrote out, and set in stone what kind of financial reality you will have. He gave you your mind, your will, and your emotions and left it up to you. You can choose to be great in any area that speaks to you. And you can certainly choose to be a wealthy fucking woman.

I love receiving more money just because I can. I personally love growing my savings and investment accounts. I love watching the money add to bigger, and more exciting, numbers. And then I love to take chunks of that money and invest into things that I desire, such as a down payment on a new property. There is no right/wrong or good/bad to how much money you allow in. You can receive as much as you choose. But until you do start to do so, you will always feel capped on what kind of life and experiences you can create for yourself. I am not here for a capped life.

HOMEWORK

Let's go deep. Free write in your journal on the following questions.

- When you think of "having more money than you know what to do with" what comes to mind for you?
- When you imagine a reality where no matter how much you spend, you earn more, how do you feel?
- What would it be like if you had already allowed in and created a life where overflow, excess, and more than enough were standard?
- What are you afraid it would mean about you if you had fuck-tons of extra money? What are you afraid would happen? How do you fear people would treat you or take advantage of you?
- What other fears do you have around becoming a wealthy AF woman?
- What in you is afraid that you couldn't handle the money or would fuck it up?
- If you had to plead the case and argue in the defense of the idea that you are meant to be wealthy, that you are allowed to, and certainly should, always have more than you know what to do with, and that you will always handle and manage it well, what would you say?

  It doesn't matter if you don't believe it's possible yet, the point is to support the side of you that knows where you are going, what you are creating, and what you will soon be believing fully when it comes to all that you are meant to have.
- Let's play with numbers. If there were $___ (large number) amount in your savings account, $___ (another large number) amount in your checking account, $___ (a possibly larger number) amount in

your investment or retirement accounts, how would you feel? What would you know? What would have become true for you?

- From the perspective of the Wealthy Woman, what do you create with all the extra you have? Where do you spend money? How do you use money? What causes do you support? Imagine spending, saving, investing, and making contributions with freedom and ease. How would this feel? Write it out.
- What does the Wealthy Woman who already lives in you have to say to you right now? Let her speak.

....

SEVEN

DEBT IS NOT THE DEVIL AND SAVING IS HOT AF

As we covered in the last chapter, saving money is essentially keeping or having some of the money you earn, make, or receive.

The majority of people feel guilty, bad, or wrong for not saving enough.

This is their dominant vibe: No matter what you are doing, you should be doing more.

Debt is another area where many people feel continually inadequate.

Like I have been saying for years: *Debt is not good or bad. Debt is a choice to pay something off over time.*

As we learned from the beginning of this book, guilt or shame—no matter how well intended—will not create lasting, sustainable change.

What Do You Fucking Want?

As long as we are basing our financial goals (or any goal) around what we've been taught we "should" do, we will perpetually live in a cycle of disconnection from what we really want.

Inside what you really want, there is the motivation to do whatever it takes.

Inside what you actually desire, there is inspired guidance.

Inside of what you long to do, there is a ton of fucking grace to get it done, do it well, and do it your way.

We have to drop the "shoulds" around money. If you want to change the patterns around what you earn, what you spend, how much you save, and the amount of debt you carry, you have to give yourself permission to be honest about how you feel and what you want.

Like I shared in the last chapter, I used to hate the idea of saving money. I hated it. I avoided it. I thought it was boring and annoying. It didn't matter that Dave Ramsey was telling the world to give up on eating out to save money or that Suzi Orman was hell bent on scaring us into coming up with an emergency fund.

A few years into starting my business, I was beginning to experience success. I was making real money for the first time in my life. I had been very intentional and diligent to develop a mindset and a belief system around money to support the creation and maintenance of this financial success. And in order to stay connected to my desires, stay motivated to create my dream life, and be able to see my own progress . . . you'd better believe I was going to focus on using, spending, and enjoying my money.

I was aware of my credit card debt. I knew I had student loans. (I gladly applied for the income contingent repayment plan each year.) And those things simply weren't the priority.

Be Honest with Yourself about *Your* Priorities

For years, I focused on earning and spending as those were my primary desires. Like I explained in the last chapter, over time I got sick of not having money in the bank and wanted something different. I had asked for guidance around my next steps. I was willing to see things differently. That opened my heart and mind and made me ready for transformation. When my friend presented the idea that a "fat bank account was hot" to me, I had a shift.

I wanted a hot bank account. (It's looking pretty sexy, present day.)

I decided that I was a woman who was into *stacking her paper* (as I called saving at the time—thank you, Beyoncé).

What I want to make clear is this: I never would have gotten here if I had forced myself to save when everything in me desired to earn and spend. And truly, I could get away with this. I was in my twenties. I had little responsibilities outside my team, my bills, and my clients. I always paid the people I was meant to pay. I always delivered the content I said I'd deliver. I was in integrity.

Had I been in a different situation, with different responsibilities, this evolution and my desires would likely have formed differently.

Many parents who I have worked with over the years have expressed desires centered around creating safety and consistency for their children. Of course, they do! That is a beautiful thing. I am consistently inspired by the men and women who generate new wealth while setting new money patterns into motion for the future generations. They are creating their desired life while establishing for their children healthy belief systems and supportive relationships with money. This not only makes a difference for their kids but changes the trajectory of the world—reestablishing who has, generates, and feels comfortable using money. I cannot think of anything more important. (Parents, I see you. And I thank you.)

Your desires don't need to look anything like mine or theirs, but you need to be clear about what they are. You must become increasingly clear on your desires.

The Most Useful Question in the World

The most useful question in the world is this: *What do you want?*

It is impossible to create what you want when you don't know what the fuck you want. We all have things we think we should want or that we believe we are supposed to want. It's time to break the pattern of looking at those for answers.

This is about tapping into your heart's desires.

If I can get you in the habit of (1) *knowing* what you want, and (2) *embodying the feelings* of already having what you want . . . then I have no doubt that every area of your life (including your finances) will continue to grow and change in beautiful ways.

Your desires, insights, and feelings are key in your decision making. Your desires are guidance. They are always indicating to you, your divinely appointed direction and action steps.

You do not have to settle simply for however life is currently going for you. You, my love, have a governing agency over your life. In psychology, we call this having an *internal locus of control*, which simply means that you acknowledge, accept, and act upon the power you have in your life.

You are the creator. Always.

You are in charge of your life. It is your continually moldable creation.

As we have already discussed: You can't receive anything that you don't believe you can have. So, feeling, seeing, thinking, and imagining what you desire as yours is the top priority.

You Aren't a Selfish Asshole

In my experience, for most of us, our desires are not as selfish as we fear they are. We are afraid that if we look at our true desires, we will find that we are a selfish, greedy, and bad person. I have yet to see that be true in any woman I have ever worked with.

What benefits you, benefits those around you.

When you have yourself in a good place, when you know you are supported, when you are in the flow of your callings, you have a positive effect on those around you. You have so much more to give when you are full, happy, abundant, and thriving.

It is safe to want what you want. It is safe to get what you want.

As I became more of a well-resourced woman, I was paying more contractors, supporting more businesses, and getting my work to more and more people.

Your abundance supports others.

This is true whether you are helping people check out at the market, obtain a mortgage, or arrive safely in your car via a ride sharing app.

Take the time to tie your work to service. See how what you do supports people. See how you being supported to support others is of the highest service to the world.

It's okay to want to feel good. It's okay to want to be happy. It's okay to want to have and make money.

I am all about you creating freedom for yourself. I am all about you having more money than you know what to do with. I am all about you evolving this area of your life.

And—in my experience—rejecting yourself, your work, and your desires will not get you there.

I want you to keep all of this in mind as we go into (drum roll) . . . the debt section of this book.

The Debt Section

I have been anticipating writing this for you.

When it comes to the story of personal finances, never has there been a villain portrayed as horrifyingly as debt.

Of course, that's only if you buy into the fully fabricated and socially enforced nonsense that says that debt is innately and always bad.

Debt is *not* a supernatural force inflicting financial ruin while sentencing you to doom and making or breaking your fiscal future.

And yes, you do get to pay off your debt.

I have helped thousands of women start and grow businesses. I have many clients who are now millionaires. I have helped people from so many backgrounds and from so many varying career paths through Money Mentality Makeover. (A woman with a traditional sales job wrote me this weekend to say she paid off her car and her credit cards during the course.)

Many of the things I teach about money and how to become financially stable—and even wildly wealthy—are completely contrary to what most other "experts" will tell you. (If you didn't notice already.)

And in line with this, it's time to tackle the proverbial monster under the bed: debt.

We have to talk about what we are thinking about debt, why we are thinking about it so much, and where to place our focus instead.

Stop Giving Debt the Power

When you stop making it mean something other than, "You spent money on things that you will now pay off over time," you can take the pressure off—off of yourself and off of what this debt means about you and your future.

Listen to me: Debt does not have any power over you or your life. It only has the power that you give it. The fact that you have debt—if you do—does not have to mean anything about you, or your worth, or future success.

Most people with debt are afraid to spend, invest, and enjoy life. They live in perpetual guilt around their debt. They feel bad or wrong that they have this debt. They feel that they are not allowed to live a happy life until the debt is gone.

Furthermore, I've seen entrepreneurs sabotage their business because they were so focused on paying off debt, that they left themselves no space to enjoy the money that was coming in or spend on themselves at all. From there, they felt little motivation to continue to create, receive, and attract money.

What's worse is that they did this under some false pretense that paying down debt would make them a "good girl" or a "responsible" adult woman.

I'll say this again: *You are good enough.*

You are worthy of your desires. *And you are worthy of the things you used a credit card or loan to obtain.* You are worthy, period.

You did not fuck it up. And you will come out on the other side, debt free. Let's just decide that right now. You aren't wrong for having it and you are also not required to have it. It is being eliminated, now.

Develop a Solid Reason for Paying Off Your Debt

Here is how I paid off my credit card debt:

- I decided not to fucking worry about it.
- I dropped every idea around how, when, and why I should pay off debt.
- I focused all my efforts on becoming more comfortable with new levels of earning and larger amounts of money sitting in my accounts. (I have watched several people manifest expenses in the exact amount of the debt they paid off, when they did not address the energetic piece of this conversation. More on that soon.)
- I decided to continually be honest with myself around the fact that I didn't actually desire to pay off the debt that badly.

I wasn't ignoring the debt. I was very aware of how much I had. (I believe in being intimate with your money.) I just wasn't making the debt mean anything. Earning and spending were my desires. I allowed myself to live my life in line with those desires.

While I did have moments of feeling guilty around having debt, and believed I was "supposed to" pay it off, my true desire was to grow my business, make a lot of money, travel the world, and purchase the things I wanted.

And that is what happened.

After the "savings is hot" convo that I have referenced a few times now, I began to access the feelings of more than enough, overflow, and extra.

For the first time, I began to feel like I would truly, truly always have more than enough.

My debt began to decrease.

Then, a solid why began to emerge for me: I wanted to buy a house in California.

After a few conversations with friends who owned property, I got clear on my desires: I wanted my debt down, my credit score up, my savings account full. Paying off debt became a deep desire that was part of a bigger vision.

Once you have a solid why, anything is possible.

My debt was eliminated within six months. (It was about $60K of credit card debt.) When I focused on earning with the intention to buy shit, that is what happened.

When I focused on earning with the intention to still buy shit, but also pay off shit, and save shit, then that is what happened.

Let's be clear: Earning more alone did not fix this. Budgeting did not fix this. Spending less did not fix this. I could have totally made more and more money and still always had a fuck ton of debt. People do that all of the time. (Often, this is because they don't feel worthy of their lifestyle.)

I could have stopped eating at restaurants I loved while no longer wearing clothes that I love and moved into some sort of restriction around spending. *That wasn't my desire.*

I love money. I love cashflow. I love receiving greater quantities of money over time. So, of course, by tying the thing I loved to debt disappearing, I had something I could truly get behind.

Overflow Eliminates Debt

My abundance naturally wiped out my debt. Having more than enough made my debt irrelevant. My overflow eliminated my debt.

There are plenty of people with great jobs that can't seem to have, keep, or save money. There are a lot of people with large incomes who worry about money day in and day out. There are plenty of good, responsible people who follow budgets but can't seem to pay down debt past a certain point or grow savings beyond a certain point.

Money isn't about numbers. Money is about energy.

You, my friend, at this point in our journey, understand vibration.

When people focus on their debt, why they had debt, how they got debt, and "Oh no! There is more debt" all the live long day, it's not shocking that their debt increases.

When you focus on money—backed with a solid reason why—of course money expands for you.

As I focused strongly on my desire to create overflow or more than enough with my intention to have the ability to buy a multimillion-dollar, beautiful California home in the future, the debt became irrelevant.

I began to have more money than I knew what to do with, so I obviously paid off the debt.

But I didn't focus on debt, I focused on overflow.

I focused on more than enough.

I focused on earning so much more than I could spend, that debt was naturally eliminated from my life and savings continually increased.

My student loans were eliminated in this way. In early 2020, I was paying bills at the end of the month per the normal. I paid off the company credit card, I paid off my personal credit card, I put money in my checking account for my personal bills, and I put money in the account my financial planner pulls from for my investment account . Usually, at this point in my process, I take what is left and put it in high-interest savings accounts. When I do this, I often have a couple hundred thousand dollars left for savings. This particular month, I had a lot more than that. To be specific, $90,000 more than that.

Something in me said, "Student loans." I felt a bit resistant, as I had been very happily on a plan I created to pay off my student loans over the next couple of years via the automatic withdrawals I had set up. I went and checked my various loan providers and learned that I had $86,000 left. I paid them off. And that was that.

When you focus on that debt, you put a lot of pressure on yourself, and continue to expand the thing that you don't even want. And when you pay it off, you will manifest the same amount of debt right back again. (This is the amount of debt that you are currently an energetic match for).

When you live, spend, act, earn, and receive from an expectation of *more money than you know what to do with*, you create something very different.

From the space of knowing that debt is decreasing for you and that overflow is the reality in which you are stepping into, let's ponder some of the potential ways this could happen for you. For example:

- If you are like me, and positive cash flow is your thing, then debt could be eliminated through overflow and increasing your income while choosing that debt gets to be eliminated.
- If you do really well with systems and structures, then maybe mapping out a plan to pay $___ off every month over X number of years is the best plan for you.

What I need you to know is this: It's your belief in the system, not the system itself, that makes it work. By believing it's working, and believing it's working for good, you'll be able to create a new reality. You will then begin to view yourself as the person who does not have debt and embody this more and more. Otherwise, this system will just become something that you tried once and only worked for a little while.

If neither of these paths are for you, that is fully and completely fine. Subsequent next steps to guide you in paying off your debt—that fit your personality, heart, and desire—will be required by vibrational law to show up for you.

Remember, the "how" of reducing your debt is not your responsibility. As you are a vibrational match for your desired outcome, all further actions present themselves to you. It is your job to be looking out for them and then take them.

Your job always: *Be a vibrational match for the thing you want.*

If you can't imagine a world where you don't have debt. Or it feels impossible for you. Or you believe this work simply can't work for you ... then you won't allow debt to be released. Like everything else: Feel the feelings of already having what you want. See it. Imagine it. Feel it. Choose to know that you are worthy of it. And then attract it. (See chapters 2, 3, and 4.) *Your job is still—and always will be—to believe.*

There isn't only one way to pay off debt. And I believe fully that you are being guided to the right steps, mindset, and "why" for you. I encourage you to give yourself permission to get clear on what you want and do it in your time and way.

Change Your Energetic Standards Around Debt

The thing is, all my credit cards have remained paid off in the years since because nothing in me has room for credit card debt anymore.

I can't imagine having it. There is simply no space in my reality. (My energetic standards around debt are a lot like the emoji of the girl with her arms crossed into an X.)

I pay off my personal and company credit cards every month.

This belief reigns true for me: *"No matter how much I spend, I earn more."*

I now have a mortgage for the home I live in in Los Angeles, as well as for my two investment properties. I feel fine about paying these things off over time.

As you know, you have an energetic minimum and maximum around everything. You have energetic setpoints. And your limiting stories, unhelpful pressure, and availability around debt can shift. Let's not focus on it, obsess about it, or let it limit your life.

Let's decide what you are meant for instead.

Money is unlimited. There are infinite ways to create more. When you're focused on how things are, how they have always been or the worst case scenario of what could happen from here, you won't have the mental, energetic or emotional space to see, feel, know, or create the alternate reality that is available for you.

Can you imagine a life where you had *more than enough*?

Think about it … more than enough to cover ALL the debt you have and still have a surplus in your bank account.

How would that feel? Can you bring those feelings into your body now? Can you feel it as *done?* Feel it as *certain?* Feel it as *complete?* Can you feel the satisfaction?

Can you see yourself saying, "I did it. I did it. I did it"?

Now, you are an energetic match for that thing.

When fear or doubt floats through your awareness, come back to this moment.

157

HOMEWORK

Get out your journal. It's time to dig in.

- **Family beliefs.** What did your parents or family teach (through words and actions or a lack thereof) you about savings? What did they teach you about debt? What else did they tell you about money? What did they teach you (or imply) about desiring money? Investing? Spending? Are their beliefs the ultimate truth?

    Of what they taught you, what do you choose to keep? What do you choose to disregard?

    Make a list of your new, aligned, beliefs.

- **Societal beliefs.** What did society teach you about savings? Debt? Money? The desire for money? Investments? Spending?

    Of what you learned, what do you choose to keep? What do you choose to disregard?

    Make a list of your new, aligned beliefs.

- **Religious beliefs.** If it applies to you, what did your church or synagogue teach you about savings? Debt? Money? The desire for money? Investments? Spending?

    Of what you've learned, what do you choose to keep? What do you choose to disregard?

- **Beliefs about race.** Is there anything about your ethnic background, skin color, community, or ancestral history that has informed you that you cannot have money or that money is not safe for you to have?

Of what you've learned, what do you choose to keep? What do you choose to disregard?

- **Beliefs about identity and ability.** Beyond sexuality, mental health, class, physical ability, intelligence, and gender, there are so many false beliefs around what is possible for us that have been created and perpetuated in our world. The question, of course, is what other beliefs have ruled you that you are ready to reform? What do you now choose?

  Make a list of your new, aligned, beliefs.

Write out your new aligned beliefs about money, savings, debt, investing, spending, and whatever else comes to mind for you.

Tweak each belief until it feels really, really good.

Deconditioning and reconditioning ourselves is a journey. Be gentle with yourself, focusing on how worthy you are. It will help to notice and celebrate each moment of progress, each aha, and all wins as you go.

EIGHT

....

NEXT-LEVEL WEALTH
PRACTICES

Here is what was required of me when I decided to become the Wealthy Woman.

My priorities shifted from: *"How much can I earn and spend?"* to: *"How much can I allow myself to have in various accounts while still earning and spending?"*

From there, my priority shifted to: *"How comfortable can I be with releasing large chunks of money from these accounts for investments, expecting that the money will be replenished through continuous earning, spending, and saving?"*

See, I was not available for financial sacrifice to create financial expansion.

As you've heard, learning to both save money and be comfortable having money was a-long-time-coming, work-in-progress kind of vibe for me. My first step was learning to receive money. My next step was letting the money add up. Once I had money in my accounts and I was increasing my ability to believe that I could have larger and larger amounts—and was unwilling to have anything less than this—a third step emerged.

I found that I needed to work on allowing myself to release or let go of some of this money. This was a whole new area for growth for me.

I had become more than a little attached to the idea of having a certain amount of cash available to me at all times. Meaning, I didn't want to take any money out of savings.

Now to be clear: You are always allowed to want what you want. If a certain level of earning, saving, spending, or investing is your desire, I want that for you. While I knew that I was allowed to desire and have certain amounts of money in my accounts, I also knew that I desired to become a wealthy woman.

To me, the Wealthy Woman is diversified. She earns money in various ways. She has plenty of resources— financial and otherwise—at her disposal. She also has her money in various containers. (I am using the word *container* to mean any place where money is stored such as investment portfolios, stocks, real estate, etc.)

She trusts herself to spend, save, release, and generate money. Let's discuss potential containers that may support you:

Retirement accounts. I had a retirement account that had a small monthly auto draft going into it starting in my late twenties. As my business grew, I began to max out (or put in the maximum allowed) each year.

First I had a Roth IRA—a retirement account for individuals who make less than a certain yearly amount. After I made too much money to qualify for a Roth IRA, I began to max out my regular IRA each year instead.

Once I realized that, as a self-employed human, it was fully up to me to prepare for retirement (as I do not have an employer matching my 401(k) plan) I began to look into other options.

With the help of our good friend Google, I learned about other retirement accounts with higher yearly limits for self-employed people.

Much like how I called GoDaddy on the phone with help setting up my website, I called Vanguard for help setting up my IRA.

Moral of the story: *No one knows how any of this works until they find out. Google it. Ask questions. Do the things.*

Later, I found a financial planner who helped me to set up some other types of retirement accounts through my company.

While I felt pretty good about this, I wanted more containers. I wanted an investment account managed by a financial planner. I also wanted a continually growing real estate portfolio. (The person who oversees your investment accounts usually oversees your retirement accounts and keeps an eye on your real estate holdings as well.)

A real estate purchase usually requires a down payment. Advantageous investment accounts my financial planner recommended required a large initial deposit. So, in order for each of these investments to become a supportive part of my financial life, I had to allow myself to release large amounts of money.

I was afraid to use the money I had saved. *What if I never make it again? What if this is a mistake? What if this is a bad investment?* I'd think to myself.

Other than releasing chunks of money to pay taxes, I had never seen large amounts of money leave an account. But, like I said, the Wealthy Woman trusts herself.

Real estate. My first two properties were purchased in my hometown. Why? It costs much less to buy there than to purchase properties in California. I know the streets and neighborhoods quite well. And a good friend of mine who still lived there had become a real estate agent. I could get my energy behind this working out in my favor. I knew I could make purchases there that I felt good about.

My experience with those two properties made the process of later buying the multimillion-dollar California home much more familiar. (I have a little vlog on YouTube that you might want to check out: "How Amanda Frances Manifested Her First House.")

I hold faith that as I hold on to my investment properties, the neighborhoods shift and change in beautiful ways, the homes themselves appreciate, the renters feel supported, and my money is safe there.

The idea here is that when you put your money into a house, it lives in the house—instead of living in a bank—and that you simply sell it at the right time to get your money back plus the profit that you will have created as the home and neighborhood appreciate.

In the $3.5 million house I purchased in 2019, every day I practice knowing that every renovation I make will support the overall value of the house. I believe these changes allow the future owners to know that this is the right house for them when I inevitably sell it for a very large profit.

Stock market and investment accounts: While I am not a stock market expert, I have been advised to invest based on the understanding that throughout the history of the American stock market, the average trends upward. While there are seasons of dips and crashes, when I invest there, my intention is to ride those times out. Like a building or land purchase, I intend not to sell without receiving my profit. I don't sell when things are down. While the money is not in my savings account, it still exists and will grow inside of the stock or bond until I transfer it back to my regular accounts.

My version of the Wealthy Woman has money in these places, feels good about it, exercises her faith inside of those containers, and continually moves forward.

Put on Your Beliefs

I decided to make some rules for how investing, and these containers work for me.

I knew that I was an energetic match for having a certain amount of money in my savings accounts, and I *put on* the belief that my accounts would bounce back to those numbers after large investments were made.

Yes, I said *put it on.*

Meaning that beliefs are kind of like pairs of pants. You can try them on, see how they feel, and see how they fit. You can continue to wear them if they work for you, your life, your body, your daily activities, etc.

You have been trying on beliefs throughout this book.

Like a tight pair of jeans, some new beliefs are uncomfortable at first, but end up working out for you after you stretch them a little. Some new beliefs are the leggings that you thought you couldn't pull off when you saw them on the rack in the yoga store but are starting to become your favorites. Some beliefs are like dress pants that need to be altered a little, but then end up fitting into your life many years after.

Instead of telling myself a limiting story that it would take a long time to build my savings back up after an investment or that I was doing something risky or dangerous, I pondered this:

What if investments don't have to feel risky?

What if my real estate properties were all always cash positive?

What if I knew all my stocks would trend upward throughout my life?

I tried on these ideas and adjusted them until they fit.

This is my vibe around investment accounts, retirement accounts, and real estate now: *"All of my accounts grow and grow. All of my investments are appreciating. It is safe to release money. It is safe to move into being the Wealthy Woman. I always win in the end."*

I am not saying that I have magical control over every person involved in every investment I make or in the stock market, banking system, or housing market as a whole. I am saying I trust myself in the overall process of becoming a wealthier and wealthier woman. I trust that I do the right things. I trust that if something were to end up being the wrong thing, I would recover. (I have already recovered in my investment accounts after the dip many of us experienced when the pandemic hit.)

I also believe this: The Wealthy Woman can always generate more money. That's who she is. That's what she does.

Per Usual: Start Now, Before You're Ready

I want to make this clear: While real estate, retirement, and other investment accounts may feel a little out of reach for you, I want to encourage you to start exploring investments now in any ways that feel good to you if expansion in this area is something you desire.

I am not saying, nor would I ever say that you are screwed in some way if you don't do this now . . . or ever. That is not how I think of life or money. I am saying that *you are capable of exploring this* before you think you are.

Like I said above, my initial deposit into my IRA each month was very small. I was in graduate school. I was balancing several jobs and had student loans. (As you know, I still had debt and very little savings.) I did not have much extra money. But this tiny investment made me feel like I was taking steps to go where I was meant to.

My initial foray into real estate was when a friend of mine had several investors going in on a small apartment building together. (This was before I bought any of my properties.)

He was accepting some very low dollar amounts to get in on this. While this might not be common, it was divine for me. Each time I listed my desires in my journal, I included my desire for real estate. When I met this friend, who had an investment group at a retreat, I knew it was divine. It still scared and stretched me, but it was my next step in an area in which I desired growth.

My first investment account to learn a little about the stock market was set up online through a website called E-Trade. I used the Google machine to read about stocks and began to play there.

I was practicing becoming the Wealthy Woman. I've always been practicing becoming the Wealthy Woman.

A Riff on the Wealthy Woman

I said this about becoming the Wealthy Woman and the experience of expanding into investing recently on a livestream:

I realized that I needed to be able to trust myself to release—I call it releasing because spending and investing just didn't feel like the right word—and truly it's not anything besides releasing. It's just letting go of a little bit of, or a lot of, money at once.

I decided to become comfortable releasing a chunk of money with the full confident intention that it would be replenished. This scared me. Like, scared the shit out of me.

But every time I release a large amount of money, I have this sense that I am simply doing the thing the Wealthy Woman does.

She trusts herself to spend. She trusts herself to save. She knows more is always available. She knows she can make it back.

She trusts herself to function at a very high level with money.

The Wealthy Woman plays at the next level before she is ready.

The Wealthy Woman elevates herself. She doesn't know how the fuck she is going to get where she is going or how the fuck it is going to work, but she keeps going.

The Wealthy Woman steps, pulls herself together, does her thing, believes it's enough so that everyone else can believe it too.

She doesn't shrink down, play small, or blame others.

The Wealthy Woman is in control of her own life.

And yet, she's obviously cocreating with God.

She's working with something—a force of love and expansion—that is much bigger than us.

She relies on this thing. She trusts that something greater is working with her, always.

She shows up. She takes responsibility for her life. And she does the damn thing.

Growth is scary, my love. Playing with large amounts of money is regularly uncomfortable for me. Not because there is anything innately uncomfortable about it or anything else, but because I am at my new edge. Areas that we desire to master or improve in will require us to hit up against new edges of what we previously thought was possible for us.

This is how expansion works.

Purchases that are very normal and comfortable today were mind-blowingly nerve-wracking five years ago.

The same is true in business and love. The next level feels a bit scary. Then you normalize it. Then you are ready for a new next level.

Over and over again.

And, like I shared with you in an earlier chapter, I believe my accounts will stay in the range of my energetic set points no matter what large investments I make.

Even after making the down payment and associated costs on my new house, along with paying my taxes, I was still above my energetic minimum in how much cash I had available. Five months later, I was 80 percent back to what I had in my accounts before I purchased the house. One year later, I have more than double the cash I did before I purchased the house. (And that's after I spent some *for-serious* money on renovations while not cutting back in any other area of my life.)

Our financial health, wealth, and evolution are meant to move forward continually.

You can handle it. You can grow financially. You can and will be led to any support you desire from real estate agents, brokers, lenders, wealth managers, and financial planners to support you. (I'd like to add quickly that you must trust yourself above all these people. You listen to their advice and opinions, but only do what you feel is right and aligned for you.)

It's up to you to expect the best, to move forward with confidence and to do the scary things as the Wealthy Woman. As you continually grow in your faith and trust in yourself, in your ability to earn, attract, and have money, and in accessing and acting upon your intuition, you will find yourself doing what is right for you.

There is no single right way to build wealth or become wealthy.

Some wealthy-as-fuck people lease homes and do not prioritize or value owning property. Some millionaires don't touch stocks. Some rich-as-hell people do not focus on earning money; they would much rather focus on multiplying the money they have through investments alone. People tend to discover they prefer one investment strategy over another by trying things out based on their job, taxes, or goals.

There are as many opinions on how to create wealth and what to do with your wealth, as there are Starbucks on random street corners in any large city.

I am not at all saying that any of my "next-level wealth practices" must apply to you. Maybe you desire to be an investor in a new company. Maybe you desire to fund projects you believe in. Maybe you desire to be a donor to organizations who could use your help. You do not have to own property or invest in the stock market. But you can if it feels good. You can if it lines up with your version of success, wealth and financial growth.

What I am saying, more than anything, is this: *Expansion is available. Wealth is maintainable. You are capable.* And you can move toward all your desires—even the ones that seem way out of reach—*right now.*

HOMEWORK

Pull out your journal. Free write on each of these Qs.

- What is your version of the Wealthy Woman?
- What types of wealth do you desire?
- If you could trust yourself fully and had the resources to do so, what kind of investments would you make?
- Above and beyond the daily spending and even the luxury spending, how do you desire releasing money to work for you? What would please you?
- What happens when you make an investment?
- What happens when you release any amount of money—large or small?
- How would having high-interest accounts growing your money for you feel?
- How would owning property that was clearly and quickly appreciating feel?
- If you had stocks and retirement accounts that were always growing, how would that feel?
- If you were an investor in a new business or project you believed in how would that feel to you?
- If you were a generous donor to a charity or organization you believed in, how would you feel?
- What are some next-level financial desires that you have, that you haven't admitted to yourself yet? When

you get to the end of your answer, ask: What else? Anything else? If there were just one more thing, what would it be?

Play with any or all of the listed questions. Focus only on what lights you up. Take the pressure off. Feel into having and using larger and larger amounts of money with ease. Feel into being the Wealthy Woman, cultivating your next iteration of growth. That is where you are going.

NINE

··

BUSINESS LIES AND
STANDARDS

From the beginning, I have been adamant that this book be a money book and not a business book.

However, I know from years of experience, that many people who begin to grasp these concepts and understand how much power they have over their financial worlds, begin to see and sense money-making opportunities more and more easily.

The opportunities were always there, but now they can see them.

Now they feel worthy of them.

Now they know they can do it.

And while plenty of people will utilize the concepts in this book without ever starting a business, many of you will likely go on to start businesses of various kinds, grow the businesses you own now, or allow yourself to receive money through business with greater ease.

When I asked my early readers what else they wanted me to share or teach on, and a few mentioned wanting to know how the concepts in this book could be applied to businesses I was hesitant at first. But upon sitting with it, I decided business concepts should definitely be included.

So, you know, I am an entrepreneur through and through. I love nothing more than the company that I own or the fact that I own it. It's mine. I grew it. I am obsessed with it.

I love how it works. I love how it serves people. I love how I set it up, what I believe about it and how Team AF and I operate inside of it.

My dedication to my work, my company, and the principles explained in this book have revolutionized my life in ways far beyond anything I could have imagined. Utilizing them to start and grow my business has been more profitable than I ever could have imagined.

That being said, this is a chapter about business and the lies we tell ourselves that limit us inside of our businesses. Some of these points are geared toward the personal development and internet marketing industries in which I operate. Some apply to businesses across industries. All of these principles convey a tone, attitude, and mindset that will transform anything you apply them to.

Lie: The Market Is Too Saturated

As I have been known to say, "The marketplace is never too saturated for those who are called." It really isn't about what other people are or aren't doing, saying, sharing, or selling. Your next steps are about what you are here to do.

As I've already asked you, if, no matter what you attempt, it would work out perfectly in every way ... what would you try? (Per usual, your core desires will contain the answers.)

Listen. It doesn't matter if someone is already doing what you want to do. They aren't you. They can't (and aren't meant to) do it *the way you will*. They don't have your spin, your voice, your take, your stories, your experiences, your revelations, perceptions, teachings, and understanding.

They aren't even *able* to do what you were created to do.

There were plenty of life coaches, business coaches, and "money mindset coaches" already out there as I was led through the phases of developing my business.

There were plenty of people with big emails lists and social media followings doing way bigger stuff than I could even dream of who were already talking about the things I wanted to talk about. And when I started sharing about the life lessons, principles, and practices that I knew to be true for me, it wasn't at all obvious that people wanted to hear what I had to say. I got crickets—lots and lots of crickets—when I first started posting about these things online.

I kept going anyway.

Just a few years later, every single day of my life, I get messages, comments, and emails from people thanking me for showing up and sharing my heart online over all of these years.

The biggest difference between then and now is this: I show up with confidence. I believe that what I have to say is important and that my gifts are of high service and worthy of massive compensation.

Say it with me: "My gifts are of high service and worthy of massive compensation."

The Book of Proverbs says it like this: "A man's gift makes room for him."[6]

The Gospel of Thomas says it like this: "If you bring forth what is within you, what you bring forth will save you. If you do not bring forth what is within you, what you do not bring forth will destroy you."[7]

Give what you have to, desire to, and long to give. Charge for it. Monetize it. Generate the cash through doing what you love or teaching how to do what you love.

When it comes to charging for your great work, I believe this: There are people out there, right now, waiting for you. They are wishing, hoping, and pleading for answers, explanations, products, and information that you are here to give. Some of them don't even know it yet but will recognize it once you create it. There is a message, product, or offering inside of you that will be the answer to someone's prayer.

Also, remember, service doesn't mean sacrifice. Do it for you because it's what *you* want to do. But know that in doing this, you will serve others.

When it didn't look like it was working, I had to know and remind myself of this, "This is all adding up in the direction of my dreams. This is all working out for me."

It turns out, people *did* want what I had to give.

And once I owned that, showed up relentlessly, and didn't give anyone a choice whether they heard from me or about me as I spread my messages all over the interwebs—everything came together.

It quickly became irrelevant who else in the industry once taught on the subjects I do now or how they were thriving when I started. Some of them are still doing the things, some have become my friends, some are nowhere to be found. It doesn't really matter what anyone else is doing. *What are you called to do?*

Stepping into a destiny you know you were always meant for is everything. Turning your passion into a career has the potential to fulfill you, give you purpose, and make you wildly happy. It will also make you question yourself, confront your deepest fears about yourself, and feel crazy as hell.

Showing up for this life and business has not been easy. Like, not even in any way. Not in the least.

But it has been worth it.

I developed my teaching style, my understanding of online branding and digital marketing, and the concepts that I am now known for, by developing and sharing them slowly as I went through my life. I was going to be oriented toward growth anyway- why would I not teach everything I learned and came to understand?

I started with nothing. Most of us start with nothing.

Like my friend and client Sara Dann says, "No one is born with a social media following."

I mean unless you are a celebrity child.

With that in mind . . .

Lie: Your Audience Isn't Big Enough

Listen, boo, I sold out my first digital course to fifteen people (grossing me $10,000) with the smallest social media following ever.

Sure, I had my personal Facebook page, but it was full of high school friends, college acquaintances and random friends of friends that I met one time or randomly friend-requested at some point.

Yet, I sold out that course using my FB personal page.

Instagram wasn't a thing yet. I didn't have a Facebook group. And no one was watching me on Twitter or YouTube.

Here is what I had going for me: I had been posting one free inspirational piece of content online each day from the day I decided to start my business. I started by posting quotes from other people. Then I began to tell stories, give lessons, and share what I was learning in life. I eventually began to give examples, lessons, and takeaways from my work with clients.

I didn't know what branding was at the time, but without knowing it, I was branding myself as a life coach with a background in therapy and a strong interest in personal development. I was teaching people how to think of me. (Hint: *That's all branding is.*)

When I took the inspired action of releasing a digital course, "Become a Life Coach," it made sense to people.

I had no plans to train coaches. It had never occurred to me to do so.

I did, however, always want to train therapists. The Ph.D. program I dropped out of was in Counselor Education—meaning for counselors who want to educate counselors.

While driving on Interstate 35 to my little sister's bridal shower a week after I sat on that rooftop pool and prayed the "God teach me how to receive money and I will teach women everywhere to do the same" prayer, I had the idea for the Become a Coach course. I outlined the modules in my head right away, released it on the internet the next week, and the rest is history.

And I did get to educate therapists after all. As therapists aren't taught much about making money in school, I've had plenty of psychologists, therapists, and counselors go through that program and speak very highly about how well I explain and teach the counseling psychology portion of our degrees to new coaches.

So, in a kind of perfect way—when it was all said and done—I got everything I wanted.

This full-circle experience occurred without an online following. It was the result of fully following my heart, holding the vision of what I wanted, asking for guidance and taking one inspired step at a time. *Wink, wink.*

Lie: I've Waited Too Long. I Wasted Too Much Time. It Can't Work Out for Me

While we are on the topic of our life experience adding up to get us everything we desire, I have another story for you.

If you didn't know, I am a trained minister. Before pursuing my Masters in Counseling and starting the Ph.D.

program I eventually dropped out of, I obtained a two-year degree from a highly regarded ministry training school. I also received a bachelor's degree from a well-known Christian University. Yes, I have *two* bible school degrees.

For many years, my intention was to be a psychologist—who worked as a therapist in the church, wrote books, held seminars and events, and taught on spirituality and emotional wellness—empowering women to live their best lives.

When it became clear that the church I had been a member of, and intern at, since I was a teenager, was becoming increasingly controlling and isolated (to a scary degree) and was no longer a healthy place for me, I ran away in the middle of the night.

I felt as though I walked away from God. (PS: God lives inside of us, not exclusively inside of a religious organization or in the four walls of a church building.) I thought I lost my salvation. I believed I had ruined everything.

I had no idea *how* I would fulfill my calling or do all the things I sensed I was meant to do with my life. I thought I was too old to be going back to school. I worried that I had wasted so much time in the pursuits that didn't work out. I felt so far behind those my age who had stuck to a traditional path in regard to their education. My confidence was shot. My anxiety was through the roof. My belief in myself was at an all-time low.

When I walked away from that world, I left a group of people who were my family, questioned (for the first time) the only belief system I had known and abandoned the path I had set myself on at the age of sixteen.

And thank God I did.

Today, I am a trained therapist. I do facilitate in-person events. I did write a book. (*Woot!* You are reading it.) I do teach on spirituality and emotional wellness. I do empower women every fucking day of my life to live *their* best lives. And my work feels very, very much like all the things I always dreamed it would.

Except I am supporting infinitely *more* people, doing way cooler shit, generating way more money, and having a way better time than I imagined. (And I am doing these things in a way that truly works for me and fits inside of my skill set, personality, and desires perfectly.)

This wouldn't have been possible if I had believed the lie that I had waited too long, was too late, or was somehow tainted by my past.

I'll say this again: It's all for your good. It's all in your favor. It's all adding up for you.

That doesn't mean that the terrible things happened in your life had to happen. It means you are now on a path of using them for your ultimate and highest good. Because you see it that way, you expect it to occur and you create it— every day, in every way, and with every decision, declaration, and breath.

It's not too late for you. You are right on time. There are big fucking plans for you. You can still do it.

Feel it. Speak it. Know it. Believe it.

The time is . . . now.

Lie: You Don't Know Where to Start or How to Niche

From a very practical sense, I fully understand that you may not know where to start.

My Become a Money-Making Coach program and Business Basics Bootcamp program were created to share exactly how to start an online, service-based business. I understand the need for this.

In another (more important) sense, you have to release the idea that you do not know what to start and just do what you fucking want to do. Say what you want to say. Share what you want to share. Teach what you want to teach.

The various aspects of your multifaceted personality, expertise, experiences, and interests are meant to come out in your work.

The biggest lie ever told to emerging businesswomen is that you have to niche yourself into a tiny box. You are the niche. You are the brand. You are the thing. And if you want to teach on or talk about more than one thing, that's okay.

For me, niching is simply unapologetically sharing the truth of my heart and strength of my work. It's my job to share about my work in such a way that the people who need one of my products, services, or offers can recognize that it's right for them. Outside of my paid offers, I feel it's my job to share content that I believe is transformative to the hearts of people. This sometimes involves politics, movements, and issues that the average public relations person would likely tell me to stay away from (mine does not). Sometimes, it simply involves the musings of my heart and channeling from the divine. At the end of the day, for me, my only job has been to use my voice for good. In that light, thinking too much about a niche seems silly.

My advice is to teach what you *most* want to teach first. Do what you *most* want to do first. And then allow it to evolve, shift, and expand over time.

That doesn't mean completely throwing out your business model and branding every other month. It means starting something, seeing it through, learning as you go, and allowing yourself to pivot and grow.

Businesses are meant to evolve and expand.

People are often afraid that they will confuse their audience by sharing about too many things. Long ago, I decided my audience was smart enough to grasp that I am a business owner who likes to travel and fashion; who teaches on internet marketing, business building, online branding, and financial empowerment; who sometimes shares her reflections about relationships, health, and family with her audience and is likely to riff on other issues she is passionate about as they arise.

This will only be confusing to your audience if it's confusing to you.

Allow who you are and what you do to become clear inside of you. All outside feedback is only a reflection of your inner confidence or doubt anyway.

Lie: You Have to Spend a Certain Amount of Money to Earn that Amount of Money

This is a lie often heavily pushed in the online coaching space.

The idea is that before you can charge a certain amount of money as a coach, you must have "invested" that amount of money on a coach.

Nonsense.

As we have already discussed, it is not uncommon for someone to spend money at a new level before she earns at a new level. Sometimes this payment, or financial exchange, supports her belief that she can now receive money at a new level.

This is not because God is up in the heavens saying, *"Thou shalt not sell a $5,000 coaching package until you have paid for a $5,000 coaching package."* This is because when you believe that you have done enough, you give yourself internal permission, and allow yourself to receive money through selling a coaching package.

Many people have bought into a belief system that says this is how it works. They have allowed themselves to receive money after they spent money and have gone on to teach this concept to their clients, further perpetuating the dynamic that this is simply how it is.

Listen to me: The value of your products and services has nothing to do with what products and services you have purchased.

Can the owner of Forever 21 not receive tens of thousands of orders until he has placed tens of thousands of orders at equivalent stores? No. And with the kind of money the owner has, he's likely hanging out at House of Bijan buying whatever the fuck he wants. (I do not actually know Do Won Chang or his shopping habits, but you get the vibe.)

When my in-person life coaching business began to pivot to an online education business, it became clear to me that there was some weird shit going on online: The person who was starting out was charging $5,000 for her business coaching while paying $10,000 for her coach's business coaching. And that person was paying her coach $20,000 for business coaching. And that person was paying her coach $50,000 for business coaching, and so on.

And many of these women had never actually run a business.

The only tactic for selling was to get online and say, "I just had my first $10,000 month!" when the person had sold two $5,000 coaching packages.

And all the coaches were spinning the story that you just had to hire a business coach and then you could start a business as a business coach, and it was . . . very bizarre. It was also very unclear what information anyone was sharing or what anyone was actually teaching his or her clients.

I can tell you this: For the vast majority of my time as a business owner, I have not had a business coach. When I've signed up to work with a coach in the past, it's been because the way a person did things represented how I felt I was meant to do things. When I feel like someone "gets" something that I don't, I want to be around them more and understand how they think, act, and operate. I may, at that time, be inspired to work with them in some form.

The price these people charge for mentorship or coaching, has nothing to do with the price I have ever charged or currently charge. For years, I charged more than I had ever paid for mentorship. Present day, I have paid one person more than I will likely ever charge.

The higher-priced coach is not the best coach for you. The coach that understands and embodies the principles from which you want to run your business, life, or relationships is the best coach for you.

Lie: The More You Charge, the More Work Is Involved

Now, I have to tell you the truth, I love selling offers at various price points.

From $7 training to $100K private coaching, I have products at so many price points.

You might imagine, that the more you charge, the more is expected of you. I have found this to be quite the opposite. My private clients (those paying for individual mentorship with me) and for those in my mastermind (a small group of women who have a group chat to support each other and also receive feedback or guidance from me) are very little work.

My private clients have the option to speak with me privately by phone weekly and my mastermind clients have the option to speak with me privately by phone monthly. Both groups have access to me through an online chat app.

Interestingly enough, these people rarely use all of their calls with me.

Those doing things at the highest level and paying the most, tend to need the least. They are essentially paying for access to me, for when they need it, but are often busy running their business and living their lives. And they didn't get to where they are (many are millionaires or multi-millionaires) by being dramatic, needy, or codependent with their mentor.

Now, that doesn't mean that those who purchase an $11 training or $197 video bundle are difficult clients. But if we were to look at percentages, it would be clear that those spending more money know how to trust themselves with their purchases and are far more even keeled as a whole.

Lie: Clients Are Difficult. Business Is Difficult. Drama Is Inevitable

Like everyone, I obviously have had difficult clients.

In addition to the information about price points shared in the last section, I have learned this: How difficult clients are is largely up to me.

There was a time where I was so desperate to prove I could make my business work that I would put up with any behavior or foolishness from any person who had paid me for anything. That is obviously no longer the case.

But what I want you to understand is that this dynamic shifted long before I had money. This shifted as I regarded my time and energy wildly valuable and set new expect-ations for how clients showed up.

Similar to the energetic set points we discussed when it comes to money in chapter three, how people treat you is about your energy. I call these *energetic boundaries*. This simply means my internal standards for how those around me respond to me.

Now, interestingly, it is very, very, very rare that I express boundaries verbally to anyone in my world. Instead, I set them internally. I decide how things go for me, how I am to be treated, what type of clients I want and am available to attract, and more.

This decision for how I am seen, treated, and respected— goes far beyond clients. I can see, sense, and feel it in how people communicate with me or my team in social media direct messages, or emails to my support team.

To put it clearly: As a whole, people don't fuck with me. Something in my energy field says, "I am not available to be messed with." This standard, decision, and expectation allows people to know how to be when it comes to interacting with me.

Now, of course, I have experienced seasons of heavy doubt and moments of internal disbelief in which I let noise and nonsense into my world. I attracted unnecessary drama and simply handled it the best I could as I realigned my standards.

If you have been available to be walked on, talked down to, intimidated, and seen as weak, that's okay. You can shift these things.

Start by deciding what kind of clients are attracted to your work and what sort of community standards you are creating. Get firm.

Set expectations for how your interactions with potential clients go. Decide that the vast majority of the time when people ask about working with you they have already decided to enroll and pay. Decide that the vast majority of clients and students in your programs love to pay you and are consistent in making their payments.

Use the process and principles in this book to feel into, imagine, and then create this reality.

Lie: Market Research Is Required

This often irritates other online marketers, but I have to tell you the truth: I very rarely survey my audience.

I wrote the following in 2017 and received a lot of interesting feedback.

> When I hear a coach or expert say to survey your audience to find out what to create/sell in your business ... I wonder how they are experiencing any fulfillment or purpose.
>
> You are not here to create what your audience thinks they want.
>
> You are here to tap into your soul, listen to your truth, and create what you feel called, pulled, drawn, led, and destined to create.
>
> My audience doesn't have any way of knowing what they need from me because it doesn't exist yet. It doesn't exist because I haven't tapped into my truth and birthed it

into the world yet. And it will never exist if I go around creating generic things that people think they want because they haven't actually grown a business yet, so they don't actually know what it takes or what they need.

YOU are the expert.

You are the expert of your content. You are the expert of what you know for sure.

I've grown a multiple-seven-figure yearly business, right?

I've grown a loyal die hard audience, right?

I have a life where I can travel the world and do whatever I want with no restriction, right?

Who knows how to do those things? Me.

Who doesn't know how to do those things or doesn't know what they need to know about those things? All the people who haven't done it yet.

Your audience is literally not qualified to tell you what they need to learn from you.

We weren't qualified to know that an iPhone would revolutionize our lives until someone made one for us.

We weren't qualified to know that cars or plumbing were needed in life until someone who knew what we didn't know showed us.

Asking your audience what they want you to create/teach/do is literally being led around by outside forces of humans who don't know what you do.

Tune into your heart.

Align with your purpose.

Create your message and content from your truth.

Ask for guidance. Take your action.

Share your heart with the world, every day.

Start now.

Say it with me: It is safe to follow my heart and my divine calling. I tap into my truth and create what I am truly here to give.

It's been quite a few years since I originally published that post, and I have to say: I was definitely on to something. I still feel this way today.

My caveat would be that sometimes I do online surveys as a way to create social media engagement, such as using the polling feature on Instagram Stories. But would not ever allow the feedback from my online community override my heart.

My internal guidance dictates my next move.

Here is a little quote from Steve Jobs:

Some people say, "Give the customers what they want." But that's not my approach. Our job is to figure out what they're going to want before they do. Henry Ford once said, "If I'd asked customers what they wanted, they would have told me, a faster horse!" People don't know what they want until you show it to them. That's why I never rely on market research. Our task is to read things that are not yet on the page.[8]

Lie: The Coaching Bubble Will Burst

As I explained above, there was some weird shit going on in the online coaching space when I got started. Some of that, obviously, had to show itself out the door.

Here is what I know to be true: We will all always desire mentorship, coaching, and guidance. Different people may receive it in various ways at various times, but I can't imagine a planet where people don't look to mentors, coaches, teachers, advisors, consultants, etc.

The coaching industry will grow and change as all industries do and a lot of nonsense will continue to be weeded out. Less-than-ethical methods and strategies will be proven to be so. And the phonies will fade away, but the personal development or self-help world is here to stay.

Lie: You Are "Taking" Money from Others When You Get Paid

I cried my eyes out the first time someone paid me for coaching. It was not very much money to them, they could afford it, and they were happy to pay it.

It was about me, and the fact that I had very little practice receiving money for the work I felt called to. I felt so guilty receiving money for something that felt so natural to me.

A lot has obviously changed since then.

Today, I don't believe that we automatically have less when we choose to spend money. I believe we often have more.

Through the act of spending or investing money, we simply exchange money for something we desire.

As I've shared, various results can be created by how we spend money and what we believe is occurring as we spend money. One option is spending knowing that more is available to you. Another option is spending as a declaration of who you are becoming and where you are going. Another is spending money that you sense will help you to earn, generate and receive more money.

In this way, no one is losing out by paying you. They are simply exchanging money for access to you, your product, a service you create, or a need you fulfill.

Your customers and clients are then able to utilize the resources, wisdom, energy, information, or presence you provide in exchange for money.

This is their choice to make. And they have the right to make choices that feel good to them.

Personally, I encourage all clients and students to follow their hearts and trust their own inner guidance when choosing to purchase one of my programs. And I trust them to do so. I do not question them around what they have felt led to purchase. I do not second-guess myself around the value of what I've created. And I do not believe I am taking anything from them when they choose to enroll in one of my courses or work with me in another capacity. I am simply providing them something they desire.

As I've been known to say a time or two, "I let people pay me. You're welcome."

Lie: You Are Responsible for Your Client's Results

Your client is the only person with autonomy or authority over her life. She is the only person capable of creating changes in her life.

Yes, you can provide her with support, direction, and guidance.

Yes, you can be wildly helpful. Go above and beyond. Overdeliver.

Yes, show up with integrity. Do and deliver what you said you would.

Yes, yes, yes. Do the right thing. Be good at your job. Do your part.

This does not make you responsible for your clients lives or results.

People are responsible for themselves.

Model, through your own decisions, direction, and action what it is like to be accountable to oneself, to show up as you said you would, and to take responsibility for yourself.

I also want to say this: *I view myself as capable. And I view my clients as capable.*

I find that when we view someone as capable, we empower them. We empower them to trust themselves, take actions that are right for them, and move forward along their own path and journey.

We disempower others when we don't trust them to do something well or do it themselves (in their time and in their way) and step in and either do it for them or attempt to control how they do it.

Whether we mean clients, romantic partners, children, or team members, I have found this philosophy transformational to relationships, business, and self-confidence. It's a practice of viewing the people in our lives as innately worthy and deeply capable.

I trust in the ability of others. I trust them to create their own way. I do not think my way is the only way. I give them space and room to figure out what works for them. I am happy to break down what works for me and exactly how I've accomplished the things I have, but I do not need them to do things my way to prove to me that I'm a good coach.

I trust them on their journey. I'm there for them as they need me. I empower them to become more self-assured and confident. And I allow them to become the women they are meant to be.

I am available to them, but I am not responsible for them. Because I know they are capable.

Lie: You Must Do Discovery Calls

There is an idea in the online coaching space that you have to book a "discovery call" with all potential clients in order for them to pay you. During this call you are meant to "overcome their objections." This basically means talking someone into working with you.

Now, it has been a very, very long time since I put myself in the position to convince someone to work with me. Most of my clients and I gave up these calls a long time ago.

When it comes to discovery calls, I discovered about four years ago that every person I got on the phone with to discuss hiring me via private coaching or joining my mastermind had already decided to work with me before the call began. Realizing this, I thought to myself, *WTF am I doing on these calls?*

There are many other options.

You can create an application to work with you. You can put this application on your website, on social media, or send it over via email. After reviewing the applications that come in, you can answer any questions the person has over email.

Alternatively, you can have a quick chat via social media DMs—using text and voice audios—with anyone who reaches out determining if you and the client are a good fit.

In either of these scenarios, you can simply conclude that the right people for your work show up certain that they desire to work with you and are ready to pay before you hear from them. Then they can reach out, ask any final questions, receive a payment link, and get started.

As a whole, my clients trust themselves. I trust myself. And truly we are all too busy to get on the phone a bunch of unnecessary times.

Of course, some people like to get on the phone to get a feel for the client. While I understand that, I can do that just as easily with a chat situation and by sending brief audio messages back and forth as I can with a phone call.

If you want to know exactly how I feel about the best way to be paid by a lot of people continually and with ease, it goes something like this: Create such a beautiful and compelling online presence, body of work, and reputation that people can't help but want to be a part of your world, happily pay you, and continually come back for more.

That's how I live.

Lie: You Don't Know How to Set Your Prices

I have been saying it for years: There are clients at every price point. For every job or service in the world there is a vast range of potential prices.

There are people who only buy lower-end goods and services. Other people look for the highest price, quality, and level of support available. And others fall somewhere in the middle.

Some people only go to Wal-Mart. Some people are very comfortable at Harry Winston.

As a business owner, pricing your goods and services is never about finding a magically perfect price point. It is about picking a price that you can believe in and stand confidently behind for the work that you provide, geared toward the type of client you desire to serve.

I very much love creating offers at various price points.

This is not a hard rule but has been a guiding factor for me: The more access a person has to me, and the more time and energy is involved in the work we are doing together, the higher the price.

Lie: That Is Simply Not How It's Done in Your Industry

Fuck what has always been done in your industry. If I had paid any attention to what was going on in my industry, I would be hosting webinars that lead to bullshit, boring funnels, relying on affiliates with big lists to sell for me, and would be so wildly dependent on Facebook ads that I would barely be profitable.

(Hence, the man I went on a date with who was claiming $900K months but spending $600K on Facebook ads while paying a very large team. After trying to convince me to do things his way, I looked at him and said, "You get that I have more money than you, right?")

Do you know what I did instead? I set a new tone for how things were done in my industry. I did it my way. I relied on sharing my heart—and creating free content—as my way to attract and engage the people who would be interested in what I had to say.

The idea of webinars made me want to die, so I created "livestream events" instead. Funnels felt like drama, so I very rarely created any. I launch all my courses through live open enrollments instead. (I have a digital course called Sell from Your Soul that breaks this down.)

I didn't do any of this because it is a fundamentally better way. I did it because it's what I wanted to do. And where you have desire—and heart leading—you will always have the motivation and drive to do the thing.

I did it daily. I did it my way. And now thousands of people look to the Amanda Frances way of doing things. I became an industry, and by doing so, I redefined an industry.

That feels much better than trying to emulate an internet marketing douche who might as well have, "Don't trust me. I don't even trust me" written across their forehead.

Speaking of, I am in an industry where refund rates and failed payment rates are often wildly high. This is true even among some very well-known entrepreneurs who boast eight-figure launches.

I remember deciding that this would never be the case for me.

While failed payments and refunds do happen on occasion, they are not as common for me as one might expect. My first $500K year, I only had one person who was delinquent in her payments by year's end. (She actually wrote in a few months later to settle things up.) This was out of hundreds of clients and course students. The next year, AFI generated $1.5 million and had less than ten people not in good standing by the end of the year.

And yes, as the company grows, I have had to increase my customer support team to help clients and students in updating their payment when their credit card number changes or expires, or when they have some sort of other issue with their recurring payment, but this is not the vast burden many online business owners make it out to be.

Here is why: I deliver what I say I will. I am consistent and reliable. And I expect the best out of the people who come into my world.

Even though there are now thousands of people enrolled in the courses my company provides, the vast, vast majority of these people desire to show up for their commitments while staying on good terms with my company, and receiving continual access and lifetime updates to the courses they enroll in. (That's right. Once they pay for the program they enroll in, they get any and every update I add to that course ...forever. That's good motivation for someone who intends to learn and grow forever. Which most of the people in my world do.)

Just because something is common in an industry, doesn't mean it has to be common in your reality.

No matter what industry you are in, I encourage you to become the standard for how things are done.

Do it your way. Do it better. Do it confidently.

People will see why it works and that it works and everything else will just be noise.

Then they'll start taking notes.

Bonus: Internet Marketing Simplified

The only way for people to know who you are and what you do, is for you to tell them.

You tell them with words. You tell them with images.

You tell them with stories. You tell them with energy.

You tell them by what you say and share, and the way you sell.

You tell them.

Over and over again.

Continually you tell them through this thing called the internet.

You magnetize them with your authenticity, conviction, and decision.

They hear you. They resonate with you. They long to work with you.

They get to know you.

Then they buy from you.

It is *that* simple.

Say it with me: I magnetize others into my world with confidence and conviction. I easily attract those who need what I have to give. My work changes lives. My presence changes lives. Who I am and how I am changes lives. I am here to be of service. I share from my heart. I sell from my soul. I do it with ease.

Lies: Selling Is Sleazy, Selfish, and Wrong

Here's the thing: Selling is the sacred vehicle by which we get people into our work.

Through selling, we are able to get people the content, goods or services they desire while being compensated for our gifts.

There is nothing shameful about calling in, sharing with, and selling to those who need your work.

I believe in the soulful art of selling. And I believe in it with everything in me.

Selling is not about being pushy, manipulative, or forceful. Nor is it convincing someone to buy something they don't need. (Gross.)

Selling is a commitment to your calling.

I am known for creating and selling programs that help women earn money.

While I've held dozens of launches that generated six figures each and have even had two seven-figure launches... I don't feel like a salesperson.

I feel like a woman on a mission with a calling who has work to do and people to reach.

For me, selling is simply letting others know about how I can help them.

Selling is how to give people the opportunity to be supported by me.

I sell with heart, passion, and authenticity.

I sell by tapping into my truth, creating inspired offers, and sharing with the world how my work can help them.

I sell by calling in and sharing with those who need what I am here to give.

Bonus: How to Handle Haters

This is the principle I need you to understand: Things people say about you bother you a lot more when you fear they are true.

When someone says something crazy about you and you know it's nonsense, you will be able to brush it off more easily. When someone says something about you and it rubs up against something in you that you have guilt, fear, or shame around, it lands differently.

The most important thing you can learn to do with negative feedback—or even online hate—is deal with the insecurities that the hate brings up in you.

The second thing I want to say is this: All negative experiences, conflict, and discomfort can be used for your good.

That doesn't mean that they were meant to happen, had to happen, or that you have to grow and get to your next level by overcoming a struggle situation.

As I have said before, "A victim story is not required to create a success story."

For many years, I would attract situations involving "haters" on repeat. These horrible situations gave me something new to overcome while providing me with motivation, or fuel, to rise into a new level of confidence, conviction, and influence. (This was exhausting.)

You get to grow and go to your next level just because you decide to. No struggle required.

However, if struggle has occurred or is occurring, you might as well turn it into gold.

The second thing I want you to understand is this: It's safe to be loved.

It is safe to be loved online. It is safe to be loved by massive amounts of people.

It is safe to accept and receive that love.

It is safe (and possible) to have a mostly conflict-free online experience as someone with a lot of eyes on them.

Some online entrepreneurs unintentionally create a dynamic where conflict, controversy, and combativeness are used to create engagement and receive love from fans defending you.

The truth is you are simply loved. Period.

HOMEWORK

What did this chapter bring up for you?

What limiting beliefs in your life or stories about you and your business did this chapter shine a light on? Let's reorganize them.

1. List them out in your journal or on your phone or computer.
2. Ask for help or guidance rearranging them. It's time we reframe these ideas. If you don't know how to ask, simply write or say, "I am available for a shift in my perspective. I am open to guidance in my path toward abundance. I welcome thoughts and ideas that deeply support me."
3. Write out new, more supportive stories and beliefs to replace the old.

Continue to journal:

- What are other takeaways you'd like to solidify in your consciousness from this chapter?
- From this book as a whole?
- Anything else?
- If there were one more thing, what would it be?
- What do you need to declare right now regarding how life, money, and business works for you?

TEN

....

BEING A GOOD PERSON +
BEING A RICH PERSON

I am experiencing a myriad of feelings as I sit down to write the final two chapters of my first book.

I feel proud, joyful, and excited.

I feel overwhelmed and anxious.

Mostly, right now, I feel conflicted.

In real-time, it is April 2020 and COVID-19 pandemic has taken the world by storm.

The economy has taken a hit, many people are out of work, and I have never been so starkly aware of the advantages that money gives me.

On a video call with my family yesterday, I said, "For nine chapters, I shared about money: earning money, saving money, having money, spending money. It mostly poured out of me. Now that I am just a few pages away from done, I can't stop thinking of what a hard time the people who don't have money are having. But I also know that those who I have worked with—who now have a healed and supportive relationship with money—are experiencing a sense of security amid a global crisis.

"I know that this work is preventative. And had they known what I teach sooner, they may have already been positioned for success in this time. This is not just about manifesting money, it's about the future you are continually setting yourself up for and the confidence and trust that serves you regardless of what is happening in the world."

My sister, who has been reading each chapter as I wrote them, proclaimed, "Absolutely."

Mom followed up with, "Amanda, that's what you tell them."

Telling You the Truth

In all of the pages before this one, I have explained the principles, broken down the truths, and poured out my heart regarding revolutionizing your relationship with money.

I know some readers will be ready to receive this information and will run with it, experiencing incredible results. I know some people may not get it right away. They may question it, try it in bits, and slowly take it in. Some people may straight up disregard it, mock it, and categorize it as nonsense.

None of the above is my responsibility.

I can give you the tools, understanding, and foundation for a life filled with beautiful experiences with money. But only *you* can choose to allow this information and energy to penetrate your heart, inform your energy, and rework your life.

As I was preparing to wrap up the book, I asked my early readers how they were doing with the content and if they had anything they wanted to ask me.

There was one question that I heard on repeat, and I sensed it needed to be addressed.

It was asked a few different ways but goes something like this: "I just want to know more about how having money feels? Can you talk about spending obscene amounts of money? What is it like to go into Chanel and buy whatever you want? What is it like to only fly first class? What is it like to have a closet of Louboutin shoes? What is it like to live without worry? To be able to afford any support you need? What does it feel like to be rich?"

I am jazzed as hell to answer this question, but here are a few things I want to cover before we go there. I will answer it fully in the final chapter.

Since the pandemic, I became more aware that being rich isn't always popular. I got into a small disagreement with my mom the other day about a CEO who was spending time on his yacht. My mom asked, "Why does he get to be a billionaire while people die on the streets?"

I replied, "Mom, my understanding is he started with nothing."

This particular billionaire was born to immigrant parents, succeeded while living with dyslexia, and started his career in the mailroom of a talent agency. He worked his way up over many decades, discovered and signed incredible artists, brought us the music of the Eagles, Joni Mitchell, and Bob Dylan, launched two record labels, produced legendary films, was ranked first on a list of the Fifty Most Powerful Gay Men and Women in the World, and since 2004 has donated 100 percent of his income to charity to the tune of hundreds of millions of dollars.

Then I told her, "He can sit on his yacht if he wants to."

I am not saying that a portion of someone's money is best spent on a yacht. (I don't feel that it is up to me to say what is aligned for others when it comes to their money.) I'm saying that there is balance in remembering the contribution, struggle, creation of those we write off as different than us. In my mind, having the resources to embrace luxury, celebrate life, and enjoy success through work we love while also making meaningful contributions is a worthy goal.

Remember: Money is not limited. And neither are we.

When you have never viewed yourself as a "rich" person or felt that wealth was a real possibility for you, you may accidently judge everyone whom you imagine that reality came easily to. I know what this is like. I have struggled with judgement toward people whom I believed had financial success that was obtained easily or handed to them. I've judged people who did not need to work as "rich kids" and "trust-fund babies."

These are not pretty parts of me. I mention this to tell you that: It's easy to take on an us-vs-them mentality when you mistakenly believe that a group of people are innately different from you at their core. All of us have love, truth, and God at our core. Our dysfunctional ways of being are not the ultimate truth of who we are—they are coping mechanisms we established to feel safe in an unpredictable world.

Here is a time my ugliness came out: A few years ago, I was on a long, first-class, international flight. It was nearly time to deplane when I noticed a woman across the aisle from me who was about my age, as she stood up to pull her designer luggage from the overhead bin. On her left hand sparkled a huge-ass ring—we're talking twenty-carat vibes.

I was plagued with judgment: *"There is no way we purchased this flight herself. Ugh, that ring. She definitely didn't buy that either. I wonder what her fiancé does. She probably comes from money. If she even has a job, she is one of those women who works for fun."*

After about forty-five seconds of this, I pulled myself together. *"Amanda! You do not know who purchased her flight. You bought this very expensive flight. She could have too! And regardless of who bought it, since you deeply desire to be in a relationship—and would not mind one bit if a man bought you a flight and a ring—you are going to have to stop judging a stranger on an airplane for seeming to have what you want."*

Looking down upon people for having what you want, is a very effective way to judge yourself out of getting what you want.

Judging people for having money is a very effective way to repel money.

If you think rich people are greedy, bad, selfish, or wrong, you won't allow yourself to become rich.

If I think being born into a financially prosperous situation is bad, I am going to create complicated relationships or sticky dynamics with my future children.

In my financial life, I have found that one of the most helpful things I can do is release the duality around the thing I want. When we want what we want, allow ourselves to want it, embrace that we want it, accept that we want it, and determine to do good with it as we receive it . . . our energy is potent. We are confident and sure. Our intentional and unintentional attractions are magnified. We are clean and clear inside of ourselves.

I wrote the following post on Facebook years ago:

Things that don't go together: Judging people for how much they spend on certain things while desiring to have those same things.

You are going to have a hard time knowing you are worthy of it, bringing in money for it, and purchasing it while telling yourself the story that it's bad or wrong to have it.

It's not bad or wrong to have things.

Things are just things.

And things cost money.

And you can choose to create a relationship with money that is supportive of you in having the things you want.

Or you can judge others and choose to believe it's wrong for them to have those things.

The problem isn't her handbag. The problem is the duality in our minds that is created from and perpetuated by not owning our desires.

Looking back, I didn't judge the rich parents of my friends, I observed them. I decided I could be like them in any way I wanted to while opting-out of any ugly things about their lives and personalities that I did not want.

For a big part of my life money was a problem. Today, money is a solution.

I have viewed myself as both a person with money and a person without money.

I was disempowered by a lack of money, and later supported and empowered by having more money than I typically know what to do with.

In both scenarios, my character and integrity was what I chose it to be.

Some people are greedy with money. Some people don't use money fairly, don't pay their people well, and take advantage of the disproportionate number of loopholes available to them. I also imagine that we don't know the whole story for every rich person who is vilified in the news.

And I know that none of this has anything to do with me.

I am fair, generous, and giving. I have integrity. I do what I say I will do.

Here is what I know: It's safe to be rich and loved. It is safe to be rich and respected. It is safe to be rich and appreciated. It's safe to be rich and generous. It's safe to be rich and anything else you want to be. It's safe to be anything along with anything else you want to be.

The night the first Covid-19 lockdown was issued in California, I sent a bonus to everyone on my online team. The amount was about an extra three weeks' worth of pay. I had been *wanting* to give bonuses and that night felt like a moment to strengthen the environment of consistency, stability, and support that is inside my company, as the world went a bit mad. This isn't something I *had* to do, but the kind of business owner I want to be.

Latching on to guilt or fear around something you have, something you were given, or something you worked your ass off to achieve will not help you use that thing well, multiply that thing, or clearly see the opportunities inside of that thing.

It's normal to experience internal conflict in life. If you are not accustomed to having more money than you know what to do with, and then begin to create wealth, you will need to reconcile and rearrange any beliefs or ideas inside you that do not support the abundant life you are creating. Or perhaps you've always had money and have always felt guilty about it. It's time to clear that up.

Use the skills in this book to identify any fear, guilt, or shame that don't serve you or support the direction you are choosing to go, rearrange them, and decide what is true for you.

Giving Back

There is a certain question I see a lot. On livestream comments, in social media direct messages, in emails—and usually from women who, like me, have a religious background.

"Amanda, do I have to tithe?"

If you don't know, tithing is giving back 10 percent of your personal or business earnings to the church, or in some belief systems, to a charity.

I love this question, because it sort of highlights our fears of being good girls, displeasing God, and fucking it up with money all at once.

Here is what has been true for me, and what I've noticed while working with thousands of women on this topic.

When giving feels good to you, it creates good results in your life.

When giving feels bad to you, it does not result in the best outcomes available.

Simply put, it is a very different energy to give out of fear or obligation than to give out of desire and generosity.

Like everything else, it is the energy with which you do the thing, and not the thing itself, that creates the results. The feelings you feel in your body, beliefs you hold in your heart, and thoughts you think as you give, tell you whether it is the aligned contribution for you.

That being said, I have found that giving when done from an overflow of love, desire and gratitude is deeply, wildly, incredibly rewarding. It feels good to give. When I donate to charity, I always feel so thankful for the opportunity to do so.

In church I heard this many times: You can't outgive God.

While, I have had seasons of giving to one particular church, and other seasons of not . . . I do have the distinct feeling that no matter where I am giving—from time to money to resources to free content online—I feel it all comes back to me.

In particular, I sense that I am compensated for the over-flow of free, inspirational content I have consistently shared on the internet for a decade. While no one directly pays me for it, I feel in my body that I am rewarded for it. And that putting it out there, while asking for nothing in return, has created divine compensation for me.

But, no, I do not believe that you *have to* tithe or give in a certain way to have a prosperous life. That is not actually how money works. Once again, money is neutral. It does not measure your worth based on morality. It responds only to your energy. As you feel good about how you earn, spend, and give—you feel safer with money. And money has a home with you. You simply are an energetically clean place to receive, have, and hold money.

Bottom line: Give freely. Receive freely. Do not worry about how your generosity will come back to you. Stay aligned with the actions that you know are right for you and notice how life takes care of you.

Becoming a Snobby Asshole

Another question I get often, from every private client I have, often as they move into the infamous six-figure month realm is this: "Amanda, what if become a snobby asshole? Is that going to happen?"

So, here is the thing. While money does make things easier, I have found that many people falsely believe that money will allow them to float around on a pink cloud of always being loved, respected and doted on anytime they are interacting with someone whom they are paying, or in a situation where they are spending a lot of money. This is not the case.

Simply put: Your friends, family, accountant, assistant, attorney, bookkeeper, and gardener will not like you if you are mean to them. Neither will the bellman, concierge, hostess, server, or doorman.

It does not matter how much money you have or are spending; people will not like you if you are a jerk face. If you ridicule people, are impatient, and are a pain in the ass, people may help you out of obligation . . . but the exchange will not feel warm and loving to either of you.

What I have found is this: If you become arrogant, ungrateful, easily discontented, and all around difficult to work with . . . the universe will attempt to realign you, fast.

Money is an amplifier. It will bring up in you the dissatisfied, demanding, and self-centered parts of you that need to heal. I can't promise you that you won't have a snotty moment, but I can tell you that with self-awareness, you will notice and desire to sort out yourself in those moments.

Life goes better when we are good to people. Life feels better when those around you know they are safe with you— when every person you encounter feels seen, respected and appreciated by you.

Money does not require you to look down upon people, but yes, if you have the tendency to do so within you, money may bring this forward to process and heal.

Taking It Deeper

I want to say something important before I go on. In spiritual and religious circles, it is often looked highly upon to *not* educate yourself, *not* stay informed, and *not* know what is going on in the world.

In the name of *love and light* or *good vibes only*, world events and other people's life experiences—that are very different than yours—are dismissed and ignored.

I suggest that we go deeper.

New ideas, concepts, understandings, experiences, and stories will rock your world. You will have to practice holding two conflicting ideas inside of yourself at once and ponder what parts of each feel true to you.

A few months back, I was watching a show called *Little Fires Everywhere*. A major theme of that show was highlighting privilege and conflict between women of color and White women; and specifically, that the areas where women of color experience oppression are often the same areas that White women are unwilling to look. In the show, a Black woman (Kerry Washington) says to a White woman (Reese Witherspoon), "You didn't make good choices. You *had* good choices."

I sat with that for weeks. Is it true that in many moments I had good choices to pick from and advantages I didn't know I had because I am white? Yes, this is true.

Is it true that marginalized people experience disadvantages that I have not always been aware of? Yes, this is true.

Is it true that a life of great choices and endless possibility was created and reinforced as I began to rearrange my identity and see myself as someone who could have success no matter where I came from, how I grew up, or what the people around me choose for themselves? Yes, this is also true.

Does the fact that I have privileges and advantages negate the fact that I worked very hard, overcame a lot, and continue to create a life many people aren't willing to do the internal and external work for? No. (I need White people to get this.)

Is it also true that as long as I thought of myself as a lower-middle-class kind of woman from Oklahoma, my self-imposed identity was blinding me from seeing the possibility of a life full of good choices? Yes, this is true too.

And the identity of lower-middle-class Oklahoman is one that I could take off, unlike ethnicity for folks of color, or ability for disabled people. My experience as a White lower-middle-class Oklahoman woman is likely very different from my Black lower-middle-class Oklahoman female counterparts.

I deeply value being able to take in new information and reconcile it into what I know to be true, expanding and deepening my views and convictions as I go.

I have to be able to hold thoughts and look at them, even if they scare me.

I can't be an informed person—much less teach manifestation well—without being willing to look at the stories, patterns, and dynamics that are already set up in the world.

Feeling negative or conflicting emotions when I look at social injustice experienced by people of color, or the economic divide between the quality of healthcare (or food) available to affluent and poor people in the United States doesn't mean I'm not being "high vibe." It means I am being an intentional creator inside of this world—someone who will do her part to unearth and unlearn systems of oppression that have contributed to the marginalization of many groups of people.

My point is this: Internal conflicts will come up.

It's safe to look at hard, weird, and distressing shit. It's safe to look at our internalized biases. It's safe to admit we have areas for growth. It's safe to lean into learning more. It's safe to acknowledge that we have room to grow. It's safe to lean into uncomfortable truths, ask hard questions, and have real conversations. It's safe to ponder ideas more deeply and fully than relying only on what we've believed up until now. This will allow us to create new worlds and realities around what we each choose for ourselves and others from here.

It isn't comfortable, but it is required if we want to mature inside of our belief systems and do our part to change the world.

An insecure person avoids uncomfortable truths. A weak person is tossed around by everyone else's views of these truths, abandoning herself as she goes. A strong and stable person is available to look at it all and sort it out inside of herself, reaching new understandings that give her clarity and direction as she goes.

The world was not set up fairly.

And I know that we are all powerful, capable, and worthy. Period.

Due to your background, past experiences, and the fuckery of oppressive systems, it may take very intentional, continual, and diligent inner work to fully believe, own, and embody this fact. These are the cards that we have been dealt. But I believe it is our collective soul assignment to play these cards differently than those who came before us.

I am firm in this: We are meant to thrive, no matter what we've been told about ourselves, our communities, people like us, or our possibilities. We are made to own our lives. We are created for greatness.

Life isn't a zero-sum game: Someone's win doesn't mean another person's loss. One person's success doesn't equal another person's suffering. This is a dominant dynamic at play in the world, and it is not the only way. It is our job to create and step into a new way.

We need people with big hearts, loads of money, and an intention to change the financial landscape of this world.

It's our job to usher in droves and give birth to generations of new rule breakers. It's time to tip the scales and create a new world of empowered people who have joyful and exciting realities with money, so we can *all* live dignified lives.

How else are we going to create a legacy of wealthy women, wealthy people of color, and wealthy LGBTQ+ humans who do their part to create a world that works for us all?

HOMEWORK

Get out your journal. You know what to do.

- Do you hold any resentments toward people who have more money than you? Are you mad at anyone who currently has something you want? How does this feel? Journal it out.
- If you trusted that you could have what they have, but in greater proportion, and purely in ways that work for you, how would you feel? Write it out.
- If you, as an empowered person with money, were not limited by the actions, attitudes, or blueprint of how other wealthy people use their money, how would that feel? What would you choose to do differently than them? What type of wealthy person do you want to be?
- If it were safe to make money even though some people with money are assholes, what would that mean for you?
- If it were possible to be a rich person and a good person, what would you allow yourself to have? What would you now know and believe about money? Is there anything in particular you'd desire to do with your money? A way you'd want to support yourself? Or to give back?

ELEVEN

....

RICH AS FUCK

I t's time for our final chapter.

The question is this: *How does it feel to be rich?*

Let's dig in.

It feels fucking fabulous. Duh.

I heard Oprah Winfrey, who is far wealthier than me, say to Larry King, *"It is a luxury beyond what everyone thinks it is, it really is. It is amazing."*[9]

I am going to say what you aren't supposed to say: Many, many problems can be solved with money.

When something needs to be fixed, repaired, replaced, or purchased in my life, if someone needs to be hired in my company, if something needs to be done around my house, I utilize money to get it done.

Unlike the many years before the past few, I no longer think that much about it, worry about it, or analyze it.

Most of the time, there is a high level of expectation and ease around money supporting me.

If something needs to be sorted and money will help sort it, then I use money to sort it.

Money is a tool. It is a resource, friend, and ally to me.

Money Exists to Support Me

One of my favorite affirmations for a very long time has been, "Money exists to support me."

As we've learned, money is a neutral resource. It has no free will of its own. It exists for the reasons you say it exists. It does what you tell it to do.

Money does not live by a moral code. Money tends to hang out with and multiply for the people who feel worthy of it. It is up to us to apply our morals and values to money, decide how we desire money to work for us, and use money well and for good.

I am sure it is clear by now that I choose to not live by any limited thinking when it comes to me, my life, my business, my career, my future, and what I'm able to have.

And when I do experience moments of doubt, dread, or fear, I know how to move through them, releasing them as I go.

My financial reality has expanded in proportion to my vision, my desire, and what I know gets to be true for me.

Here are some ways having more money than I know what to do with has affected my life.

Health. Late last year, when I had a severe allergic reaction to an antibiotic after a procedure, my close friends had been checking on me around the clock. I had a rash from head to toe and a very high fever. I knew my friends had families to worry about and holiday plans to enjoy. I needed a solution that would support me and hopefully take the pressure and worry off those I love.

I paid a nurse her daily rate to oversee my meds, drive me to appointments, and communicate with my doctor around my progress. She even made me soup each day. I was so thankful for this incredible woman and her help at that time.

In another instance, I couldn't breathe one night and had a bit of chest pains, I Googled "in-home doctor" for my neighborhood. The dispatcher called a doctor. He came over within an hour, checked my vitals, listened to my symptoms, and diagnosed me with indigestion and allergies, and checked on me every day for a week.

Did you know you can have chest pains when you just need to burp? lol

In a world where health-care costs are astronomical, and in a time in which leaving your home while sick could endanger others, I was thankful to not have to schedule an appointment, drive anywhere, sit in a waiting room, fill out forms, talk to front-desk people, or wait for results. He just came over.

The world isn't fair. It is not set up to give all people the help that they need. But as we redistribute funds to those of us who care about progress and change, we even the financial playing field. We lift others up with us. The fact that I had the means to pay for this in-home doctor's visit with ease and receive attentive medical care late at night reminds me of why I do this work—to support you in getting the power of money in your hands so that you can protect, provide, and care for yourself and others without stress or strain.

The simple truth is money changes things. Through the work I share, I have seen very "regular" people revolutionize their lives through the work they've done around their perception of their worth, power, potential, and destiny.

I am one of those people.

Fashion. Oh, how things have changed for me in this area. I was a girl who felt tremendous imposter syndrome inside a Chanel boutique. I am now a woman who is equally as comfortable leaving the store with several things she loves, or leaving empty-handed if nothing has caught my eye.

This has been a process for me. The first three Chanel bags I bought were vintage and located at resale shops. I wasn't automatically comfortable marching into the stores I now love the very first day I could afford to.

To be honest with you, those first few purchases were weird for me! I had work to do to become comfortable with owning beautiful things and to trust myself to take care of these things.

I have had more than one client, whom after purchasing a luxury item, temporarily lost or damaged the item. She wasn't yet comfortable having it. She didn't yet feel safe with it. She didn't trust herself with it. And she created a scenario to allow her to work through this. I have helped these women to create secure and unattached relationships with their possessions.

While I am aware that if something were to get lost or ruined, I could afford to buy another or get it fixed because I have little fear left in this area ... I keep many things for years and years. It feels good to take care of my things knowing they take care of me in their unique ways. I have a tailor, cobbler, and drycleaner that support these efforts.

My possessions feel meaningful and meaningless at once. Things are just things. I am in many ways unattached. However, I view my material belongings as very pretty symbols of my growth, progress, and accomplishments.

That being said, I feel safe to get rid of things when they no longer serve me. I do not keep things "just in case" for fear that I cannot buy another.

Today, I purchase quality items that last. These are the things I love. And I feel good consuming little-to-no fast-fashion that relies on the labor of unfairly compensated workers to create a profit.

When I am done with something, I give it away or sell it. When I sell it, I typically donate the proceeds to charity. Disposable clothes are no longer a part of my life. I buy quality clothes intentionally. I release them when I am done. This creates less waste while also supporting organizations I believe in.

There is also a bit of lightheartedness in my shopping experience.

When I like both pairs of shoes, I feel comfortable getting both.

When I like a pair of workout pants and find that I am wearing them often, I sometimes purchase another color or two available or order a second pair of the color I've been wearing regularly. I've even grabbed the coordinating sports bras, tennis shoes, or scrunchies to go with them.

There are times where the wardrobe up-level has blown my mind.

Once on New Year's Eve, I added up the cost of the dress, shoes, coat, bag, and jewelry I had on. Now, I wouldn't normally have my most expensive coat, all of my favorite jewelry, crystal boots, and a designer dress on all at once, but that day I did. And while most of these items were acquired one at a time over a long period of time, on that particular occasion I had on $133,000-worth of items at once. I was baffled with and impressed by and proud of myself at once. I was also a bit embarrassed.

It felt unfair—and even unheard of—compared to my old life. I understood, logically, how I had gotten to this moment, wearing this outfit. I didn't feel unworthy or like I didn't deserve it, but I felt the contrast of both the life of my former self and of all the people for whom $133,000 is a dream salary. I feel like a regular person, a normal girl from Oklahoma. I'm not special.

This moment drove home for me why I do what I do, why I teach about money, and why I share everything I know. I don't have secrets when it comes to money. Money is not some elusive club. I do this work so that others can rise into their highest potential and go far, far beyond me and what I have achieved thus far. Learning to be unapologetically in my power when faced with moments like this has been key to embodying my work and owning my continual financial expansion.

Most days I feel proud of what I have and what I have created and very aware of where I came from and what I didn't used to have . . . all at once.

Home. We have already talked a lot about buying my home, renovations, down payment, and everything the above brought up for me, but a few more home-related things come up to share with you.

The other day, I was on the phone with a woman whom I mentor, who was processing some conflicting emotions as she created her first seven-figure year. Walking around my living room, talking to my client, helping her confront some of her fears around going bigger, I said, "Love, I get it, I have individual pillows on my couch that cost more than my rent five years ago."

As I said it, I couldn't believe it was true. They are really, really beautiful pillows. lol

As a single woman living alone there have been times when I haven't felt safe in my homes. I believe in creating a sense of safety both in myself internally and through my external practical actions. That being said, the cost of my home automation and home security was a bit more than I used to make in a year, about six years ago. This contributes to my feeling safe and supported in my home. I am so happy to be able to provide myself with this feeling and experience.

Sometimes moments of spending a lot of money feels exhilarating. Sometimes I am in awe, disbelief, and excitement. More and more over time, it begins to feel standard for me, which is how I know I have normalized it.

And normalizing one level is required to go to the next one. And normalizing what you don't have yet, helps you to receive it faster.

But, to tell you the whole story, I have had many, many moments of looking around realizing that I've made it while thanking God and weeping.

The Team. I have a business manager, an operations person who is also a tech genius, a virtual assistant, a social media manager, a graphic designer, and others who support my online business. I have a yard guy, a pool guy, a handyman, a cleaning lady, and a personal assistant who support me around my home. Some are people who I have worked with for over five years! They are family. They are friends. I love them so much.

I have had to become more and more comfortable with people helping me. I have not always felt safe letting people help me. I have had to release control. I have had to view those around me as wildly capable and better at their work than I could be. I have had to learn that when it comes to tasks I do not thrive in, there is someone out there who will love and be perfectly cut out for doing that work.

It is my job to pay them well.

I couldn't do what I do, or do it brilliantly, if I didn't have a team around me made up of people who each do their jobs brilliantly.

My online team is almost always entirely made up of women. There have been a few times over the years when I realized nearly every person on my team was a single mom. This was not done on purpose, but it does make sense that manifested this as the entire purpose of my life is supporting women. The team reflects my heart, desires, and values. It feels so good to support the women on my team who dedicate themselves to work they love, and in return are providing for their families.

By combining their gifts and skills with mine, we create a mission and movement bigger than ourselves.

Travel. I haven't flown economy in a very long time. To take it a step further, I avoid at all costs business-class flights that do not have beds that lay flat. By trial and error, and by studying seat maps, I have learned to spot which flights, at which times, to which cities have first/business-class suites with seats that recline into beds.

I learned years ago that waking up in a new city refreshed, after a full night of airplane sleep, a good meal or two, and a relaxing movie—puts me in the position to continue to run my company with a clear head when I land.

This is nonnegotiable to me, but it was a process. First, I selected economy-plus when planning my travels. Then I manifested a few first-class upgrades. Eventually, I purchased lay-flat beds for long flights, but spent hours making sure it was the least expensive first-class flight available.

Over time, my standards increased. I tried out a private jet service for a year and finally found my way to my preferred airline, in which I have allowed my points to add up and am now at the highest level of that airline's loyalty program. (Which I think is kind of cool!)

I sometimes have a driver waiting to get me to and from the airport. Sometimes, I think it's more fun to Uber or figure out the public transportation in that city. I know it is not required that I do the fancy thing, and sometimes it feels really good to let my adventurous, wandering traveler side of me roam freely.

That being said, I love a beautiful, grand, five-star hotel. I love the way I am greeted at the door. I love when the staff remembers my name—both when I return from a day out and when I come back years later. I love the towels, sheets, pillows, view, room service, and overall experience.

Because I book with my American Express Platinum credit card, I am guaranteed an early check-in, late check-out, and free room service breakfast. It also sometimes comes with a drink upon arrival and a credit to be used at the spa. I've never been mad at a spa credit in my life.

Like I've said, things that once felt extravagant, become standard. I think that's part of financial growth. But they do not have to stop feeling good. And you do not ever have to stop being grateful. Standard does not mean you don't love them. It just means you know you are worthy of them. It means you've become comfortable and confident being supported in this way.

Food. I really like food.

I also like restaurants. And eating out. And ordering in. A lot.

Growing up, I was taught that we must limit eating out, as eating at home cost far less than eating at a restaurant. I internalized this and felt guilty for longing for the dining experiences I loved.

Today, I have a very different mindset.

I know that it's important that my body is nourished. I know that eating out is also a time where my soul is nourished by the humans I dine with and the conversations we share.

I no longer feel guilt for "eating out too much" or spending money on food. In fact, I have even felt mildly disappointed when a nice dinner costs less than I was planning to spend on my family or guests. I was a server in bible college I love to tip very well.

Also, I really, really love tiny, local gourmet grocers. Higher-priced items are part of the experience in these markets. I don't mind it at all. The aesthetic, quality, and service create the vibration I desire to be in. I am very intentional to place myself in places that feel good—grocery stores included.

Ease of mind. Over time, I've felt more and more that price comparing is not always the best use of my time. I know that by paying for convenience or speed, I am really paying for time, space, and freedom.

In this way, delivery fees, shipping fees, rush fees, or service fees are sometimes worth it to me.

Through a delivery fee, for example, I am saving myself the time and energy it would take to go to a store. I am essentially buying myself time. This time can then be devoted toward whatever I desire to focus on—passions, work, recharging, quality time with friends and loved ones, and so on.

I feel free to use money for whatever I need. Money is a tool—a tool meant to support me in whatever is important to me. I use money strategically and intentionally. And I leverage it toward my mission, purpose, and desires.

Bottom line: I allow money to create ease, space, and freedom in all areas of my life.

It's pretty fucking great.

The Limitations We Create

Wealth is a relative thing.

There is someone wealthier than almost everybody. And everyone has one perceived limitation or another—whether self-imposed or not.

What are my self-imposed limitations these days? Well, while I feel completely comfortable spending several hundred dollars on a pair of designer shoes or two (or maybe even three) during one visit to a store—I wouldn't buy twelve. I have the money in the bank to buy 5,000 pairs of shoes, but that really isn't the point. The point is to feel good about how I spend and use money.

There is a version of excessive that feels abundant, a version of excessive that can feel wasteful, and a version of excessive that says to me that someone isn't yet comfortable allowing money to sit in an account without being spent.

Now, I don't really believe in "wasting" money. I believe only in using money in ways that do or don't support you, feel good to you, or work for you. That being said, I still have my self-created limits and boundaries that exist as guidance around what I have discovered works for me. Five thousand new designer shoes simply does not work for me. I love having money in the bank. I love having money left over. As we've covered, I love both having money and spending money in increasing proportions.

And yet, I still get a sinking feeling in my stomach when I go to pay for something I *don't* really love or don't really want.

In some ways, it feels like money changes everything and nothing all at once. I still have to process doubts and fears. I still have to choose my path and trust myself. I still have to decide who I am becoming. I just look at and work with higher price points now.

I once said to a personal assistant, who carries my credit cards in her wallet, "Listen, none of this came by accident. When I spend money, I do so on purpose."

While changing your mindset will help you make more money—on its own, making more money does not change your mindset. (We have all met a rich person who still acts and feels poor as fuck.)

However, the Wealthy Woman spends, and she spends well. She feels good about what she spends. *She has nothing to prove through how she spends.* She buys what she wants, and she leaves the rest. And she doesn't worry too much of any of it.

She left the world of compensating and proving long ago.

She trusts herself to have it, so she has no need to spend all of it.

If she were led to release it all, then she'd trust herself inside of that too.

She is not responsible for the sake of responsibility, but she knows that by honoring her money, she honors herself.

Levels and Layers of Wealth

I am aware that the dollar amounts I earn, spend, save, and circulate are wild. I also know these amounts are nothing to someone who is worth several hundreds of millions—or billions—of dollars.

To give myself perspective, I sometimes consider this: A low-end jet costs $2 million. A high-end yacht costs $250 million. When I didn't have money, $1 million, $10 million and $100 million all sounded pretty close to the same thing. Once, I had millions coming into my life, I realized that there are many levels of wealth that I did not previously see.

Having a few million at your disposal and being a legitimate billionaire are not really the same thing.

While I don't view any amount of financial abundance as out of reach, I am aware that the levels and layers of wealth go on forever. I do not feel I am required to get to some specific financial level, but I do practice viewing all levels as available.

So, I don't have a yacht. I don't own luxury vacation properties around the world. I don't have a jet. I don't own, lease, or even timeshare a plane, boat, or island of any kind at all.

But if or when I desire these things, I will pursue them. I believe it is safe to do so.

Some of the above I could own or invest in now. Some of these seem a bit of a reach at this time and are not yet a focus for me—but could be obtained through learning more, getting clear, earning more, and setting my goals accordingly. And I will work the principles in this book to get there as led by desire.

Nothing is innately out of reach. Everything is possible.

Money Feels

To get back to our question, having money feels amazing. It's relaxing and relieving. It feels like safety. It feels like security. It feels like home. It feels comforting and supportive.

It feels like joy and gratitude. It feels like hard work adding up. It feels like an intention coming to fruition. It feels like what I have felt, observed, suspected, and worked with coming together more easily and impactfully than I could have imagined.

It feels like desire, receiving, embracing, choosing, and allowing in. It feels like being tuned into the thing you want, leaning back and letting it in.

It feels fucking good.

It feels expansive. It feels like endless possibilities. It feels open, willing, and ready to help me.

It feels normal, expected, and required.

I feel well resourced. I feel appreciated and supported by money. I feel like I have an advocate and ally in money. I feel held. I feel adored. I feel loved.

And remember: Money can't feel like anything on its own. It can only reflect and magnify back to us our feelings about it.

It feels how you decide it does. You bring these feelings into your body to create this.

I allow it. I welcome it. I love it.

I make space for it. I regard it highly. I do not entertain ideas that are unsupportive in regard to me having it.

I have fully reorganized how I work with money, how money works for me, the rules at play, and the paradigms I operate in.

Because of this ...

Today, I feel, know, and literally have more money than I know what to do with.

More Money Than You Know What to Do With

The funny thing about deciding and stepping into having more money than you know what to do with is that you will find things to do with it. And I mean *all* of it. (Even when the only thing you desire to do with it is have it sit in the bank and be ready to support you upon the next endeavor that requires a big chunk of it.)

Reaching a place of using it all, or of needing or wanting more money (or more of anything) does not mean you are doing it wrong; it means *you are being called upon to expand.*

You will expand into new realms of generating, spending, saving, having, and investing as you engage in the journey outlined in this book.

Throughout my career, as I decide it's time for my next level of earning, strangers on the internet act like something must be going wrong when I elevate into making more. I've read that means that I must be irresponsible with money. Or that "her spending must be out of control."

The truth is, money is available, and I like having a lot of it.

I let it be *the* thing. Not the *only* thing I focus on, love, appreciate, or do inner work around—but something that I am *always* willing to focus on, love, appreciate and do inner work around.

I show up for it—and it shows up for me.

My job is to want it and know I can have it—and remove or reconcile anything in me that is in opposition of these two things. Money's job is to come to me, stay with me, support me, and do whatever I tell it to do, want it to do, or need it to do.

As you become comfortable with, accepting of, and fully available for one level, the next opens up for you to step up and into. Over and over again.

New limiting beliefs—or deeper layers of previously looked at limiting beliefs—come up to be healed, and you begin again, this time with more knowledge and awareness of the process.

I am confronted with my personal perceived limits when I receive or release more money than ever before. I feel my financial capacities expanding—sometimes uncomfortably—in these times.

Money supports me in my growth and on my journey, as I step further into who I am and who I was always meant to be.

As I've expressed countless times now: The possibilities for you are endless. There is no cap on what you can have, do, generate, create, become, and be.

You truly were made for greatness.

Your desires are, in fact, guiding you.

You were created for the best fucking life. You were made to have it all.

You really can do it.

And your next level awaits.

So, go get it.

HOMEWORK

Free write.

Topic: What does it feel like to have money? Write it out in first person, present tense. Write it as though it has already happened to you. It is here. It is now. It is yours. Feel it in your body, mind, heart, and energy.

Next, declare who you are, what you choose to have, how you choose to be, where you are going, and how it is all meant to be for you.

What are you deciding, choosing, and taking away from this book? If you've written it out, write it again. You will find it gets clearer and is backed with stronger energy and emotion, as you go. Write from an energy of deciding, declaring, and knowing. Put doubt aside and do your thing.

You may want to list any sayings, takeaways, affirmations, or truths that you are ready to integrate and allow to become more real for you.

Once you are finished, say it with me:

RICH AS F*CK

THIS IS WHO THE FUCK I AM.
AND WHO THE FUCK I'M MEANT TO BE.
THERE IS NO HOLDING BACK.
I CHOOSE TO BECOME ... AND RECEIVE.

ACKNOWLEDGMENTS

Mom—Thank you for birthing me, for believing in me, loving me deeply and for telling me I could do anything I put my mind to. I believed you.

Dad—Thank you for being our rock and consistent and stable presence of strength and love. You are the best man.

Andrea—You are the greatest gift of my life. I am so happy God gave me you and that I have the privilege of being your big sister. Thank you for fighting the trolls, for all of our sister things, and for being you. I am so proud of you. I have your back forever.

Monica—Thank you for taking care of your little sister (me) so well. From the Barbie house to the mail to the place to stay when I needed it. And for being so completely delightful. I love you so much.

Meaghan—Thank you for supporting me during so many growing pains. You are such a beautiful soul and I appreciate your role and how you helped us grow while it was aligned so much.

Baby—Thank you for being such a good fucking man, a force of calm, and a grounding presence in my life. Thank you for all the things you do for me, and to me, so well and all the ways you love me—big and small. I am happy the rare earth magnets inside of us made you chase me down the street that night. I appreciate you endlessly.

Deb Rebar—You do the things, know the things, sort the things, oversee the things, and take way more off my plate than I can even fathom. You make it all work. Thank you for being our operations woman, tech guru, voice of reason, and business mom. Thank you for your integrity, for listening, and for being a rock solid human being.

Kim Hamilton—I just adore you. Thank you for having my back all the livelong day. You do so much for me, the team, and our community. You support us all so well. I am so happy you pitched me the DMs that day.

Bondie Metchore—You are such a powerful, kind-hearted, loving, generous, incredible woman. We have been through a fucking lot. I can't tell you how much it means to me that you pray for me. I thank God for you. Thank you for all you do.

Brynna Nicole—OMG! The countless graphics, website elements, sales page components, social media covers, etc. Thank you for your creativity, for making everything so pretty, and for analyzing so many shades of pink with me—over and over again on repeat. lol

Kaci Ally—Thank you for your wisdom, passion, and knowledge around diversity and equity. Thank you for your brain and feedback. Thank you for helping Team AF in the ways you do.

Andrea Crowder—Thank you for being my second reader and incredible friend. Thank you for calling it the "Money Bible" when I was so freaked out about writing it. Thank you for always having my back and for being you.

The Early Readers—Thank you for signing up to read this crazy book in real time. Thank you for being on this journey with me. Thank you for your love, feedback, and testimonials. I love you. It was such an honor to have you with me as I wrote my first book.

Sarah Love—You are the wildest, most loving, most startling, most compelling, most effective healer I know. Thank you for the worlds you build, the paradigms you rearrange, the bullshit you collapse, and your continual work. I love you.

My private and mastermind clients—You bring me alive and remind me why I am here. I honor your journeys, your path, your commitment, your courage, and the way you are redefining life for the generations that come after you. You are the game changers.

The MMM Money Mavens—Thank you for listing. Thank you for investing. Thank you for engaging. Thank you for trusting. Thank you for believing in me and yourself. Your success stories are the thrill of my heart and the evidence of my life's work.

Cara Alwill—Thank you for forcing me to write a book. lol. I love you. I am inspired by you. I am proud of you. I am thankful for you. Thank you for who you are and what you do.

Gabby Bernstein—I thank God for the day I saw your book on the shelf. It changed everything for me. I pray this book is exactly *that* for those whom it's meant to serve.

Rebecca Caccavo—I thank God for you. I am so happy that you came into my life at the perfect time and most uncomfortable way and helped me add the final pieces that were truly needed. Thank you for your nuance and depth. Thank you for both/and. Thank you for what you pulled out of me. I appreciate you!

Cara Lockwood—Thank you for seeing and understanding my voice. Thank you for your belief and confidence in the book. Your feedback helped me to move out of my resistance and into trust right when I needed it! Thank you!

Stephanie Gunning—Thank you for your beautiful formatting, incredible way with words, and final polishing of this book. I appreciate your works so much!

CITATIONS

1. Carl R. Rogers. *On Becoming a Person: A Therapist's View of Psychotherapy* (New York: Houghton Mifflin Company, 1961), p. 389.

2. Proverbs 18:16. The actual passage reads: "A man's gift maketh room for him, and bringeth him before great men." *King James Bible* (1611).

3. Ephesians 3:20. *New King James Version* (Nashville, TN.: Thomas Nelson, 1982).

4. The actual passage from 2 Corinthians 12:9 reads: ". . . 'My grace is sufficient for you, for My power is made perfect in weakness.' Therefore most gladly I will rather boast in my infirmities, that the power of Christ may rest upon me." *New King James Version* (Nashville, TN.: Thomas Nelson, 1982)

5. Wayne Dyer. *The Power of Intention: Learning to Co-Create Your World Your Way* (Carlsbad, CA.: Hay House, 2005).

6. Proverbs 18:16.

7. *The Gospel of Thomas* was recovered in Egypt in 1945 as part of a collection of thirteen codices, containing fragments of fifty-two early Christian and Gnostic texts, collectively known as the Nag Hammadi Library after the town they were found in, stored hidden in sealed jars. The author of this gospel is Didymus Judas Thomas, aka "Doubting Thomas," who heard these words spoken by Jesus Christ in his presence.

8. Walter Isaacson. *Steve Jobs* (New York: Simon & Schuster, 2011).

9. Oprah. *Larry King Show*, CNN.

RESOURCES

Programs

Money Mentality Makeover: Seven modules. Twenty-two bonus videos. Designed to carry you for money manifesting foundational principles to quantum wealth concepts. Meant to be the only course on money you will ever need. Bonuses include the Elevate into Overflow five-video series. You receive all content and all future updates, for life.

Drop the Money Struggle Bundle: A ten-video foundational training bundle on money. Good for clearing past money fear, forgiving past money history, identifying limiting beliefs about money, and establishing a supportive relationship with money. Videos include: *The Art of Shifting Quickly*, *Money: A Game You Play*, *The Incremental Increase*, and more. Homework and affirmations included.

Energy and Frequency of Money Bundle: A seven-video training bundle. Fast-paced and fun. Videos on the vibration of abundance, relaxed receptivity, eliminating debt, energetics of continual financial increase, and setting new rules and standards around money. Homework and affirmations included.

Start with whichever program motivates you to get started now.

Please note that both the EFM and DTMS are included in MMM. Because of this, if you are enrolled in either of these bundles, you receive your money back in the form of a coupon code toward MMM during future enrollments.

Business Basics Bootcamp: Four-part video series designed to give you the confidence, know-how and initial steps in starting a business. Videos include *The Practical and Energetic Steps for Starting a Business, Attracting Soulmate Clients with Ease, Showing Up Online While Showing Up for Your Destiny,* and *The Energy of Manifesting Your Dream Business.*

Not seeing what you are looking for? Dozens and dozens of online trainings, courses, and video bundles—on topics such as financial empowerment, spiritually aligned business, online marketing and more—can be found at https://amandafrances.com.

Free Resources

Money Mentality Free Resources: Content that has been created over many years and compiled for you to support you in developing and embodying belief systems (ways of thinking and being) that aid in your financial growth. Includes two money meditations, a two-hour "Manifest Money Now" party and a three-part video series on "Breaking Your Blocks" around money. When you sign up for this content you also receive a special price on MMM during

our next enrollment period:
https://amandafrances.com/money-wait-list.

Boss Lady Meditation Series: Meditations created over several years and compiled in one place for you. Includes the *Wealthy Woman Meditation, Earn with Your Divine Purpose Meditation, I Am Enough Meditation, Manifest Your Desires Meditation, Calling in the Cash Money Meditation,* and many more: https://amandafrances.com/boss-lady-meditation.

Podcast: *And She Rises the Fuck Up* **with Amanda Frances:** This is a podcast for the woman who desires the income, impact, intimacy, and influence she was born for. Through practical advice, spiritual solutions, and energetic principles, Amanda helps women to achieve their wildest dreams in business, life, and love. This is a must-listen for the woman who refuses to hold back, shrink down, or play small any longer. Available on iTunes, Spotify, Stitcher, and many other podcast providers.

Social Media

Instagram: https://instagram.com/xoamandafrances
Facebook: https://facebook.com/xoamandafrances
Pinterest: https://pinterest.com/xoamandafrances
YouTube: https://youtube.com/amandafrancesxo
Twitter: https://twitter.com/xoamandafrances

ABOUT THE AUTHOR

AMANDA FRANCES is a world-renowned thought leader on financial empowerment for women. In the world of personal development, she is widely known as the "Money Queen." Through her wildly popular digital courses, highly engaging online presence, the weekly "And She Rises" podcast, an ongoing mastermind for women entrepreneurs, and her daily free inspirational posts, meditations, and videos distributed across her social media channels, she empowers women to design lives and businesses they are wildly obsessed with. She has written for *Forbes, Business*

Insider, and *Success Magazine.* Her mission is to get the power of money into the hands of goodhearted women who are here to change the world.

Combining a background in ministry as well as mental health counseling with practical business advice and a deep knowledge of spiritual and energetic principles, Amanda isn't quite like any other "money coach" or "business guru" you've encountered. A true self-made women, while putting herself through graduate school, Amanda taught herself how to build her first website.

Nine years later, Amanda Frances Inc. is an eight-figure global brand with users in ninety-nine countries and clients in eighty-five countries. She credits her success to her sheer determination, a deep desire to serve others, and an unwavering belief in her own dreams.
Amanda put herself through school, earning a master of science in counseling degree from Southern Methodist University and a bachelor of art in psychology from Oral Roberts University.

She is a native of Tulsa, Oklahoma, but in July 2016, she put everything in storage and took off to see the world before buying a home in West Hollywood, California, in late 2019.

Made in the USA
Las Vegas, NV
06 March 2021

19110837R00154